30 Minute Italian

30 Minute Italian

Cook modern recipes in
30 minutes or under
using Arborio Rice,
Polenta, Porcini, Morels,
Orzo, Linguine, Fontina,
Pecorino, Pancetta,
Marsala, Cavolo Nero,
Truffle Oil, Pumpkin
Seed Oil, Saffron, and
Balsamic Vinegar.

Fran Warde

Photography by David Loftus

LAUREL
GLEN

Published in 2000 by
Laurel Glen Publishing
An imprint of the Advantage Publishers Group
5880 Oberlin Drive, San Diego, CA 92121-4794
www.advantagebooksonline.com

All notations of errors or omissions should be
addressed to Laurel Glen Publishing, editorial
department, at the above address. All other
correspondence (author inquiries, permissions
and rights) concerning the content of this book
should be addressed to Hamlyn, an imprint of
Octopus Publishing Group Limited,
2–4 Heron Quays, London E14 4JP.

ISBN   1-57145-673-2 (hardcover)
        1-57145-679-1 (trade paperback)

Library of Congress Cataloging-in-Publication Data
available upon request.

Printed in China.

1 2 3 4 5   00 01 02 03 04

Main text set in 8½ on 12pt Arial and
Monotype Grotesque Light.

Publishing Director: Laura Bamford
Commissioning Editor: Nicola Hill
Editors: Anne Crane and Katey Day
Art Director: Keith Martin
Executive Art Editor: Mark Stevens
Designer: Peter Gerrish
Photographer: David Loftus
Home Economist: Fran Warde
Stylist: Wei Tang
Indexer: Hilary Bird
Production Controller: Katherine Hockley

North American Edition
Publisher Allen Orso
Managing Editor JoAnn Padgett
Project Editor Elizabeth McNulty

Notes

1. Standard level spoon measurements are used in
   all recipes.
   1 tablespoon = one 15 ml spoon
   1 teaspoon = one 5 ml spoon
2. Eggs should be medium unless otherwise stated.
   The USDA advises that eggs should not be
   consumed raw. This book contains dishes made
   with raw or lightly cooked eggs. It is prudent for
   more vulnerable people, such as pregnant and
   nursing mothers, invalids, the elderly, babies,
   and young children, to avoid uncooked or lightly
   cooked dishes made with eggs. Once prepared,
   these dishes should be kept refreigerated and
   used promptly.
3. Milk should be full fat unless otherwise stated.
4. Fresh herbs should be used unless otherwise
   stated. If unavailable use dried herbs as an
   alternative but halve the quantities stated.
5. Pepper should be freshly ground black pepper
   untless otherwise stated.
6. Ovens should be preheated to the specified
   temperature —if using a convection oven, follow
   the manufacturer's instructions for adjusting the
   time and temperature.
7. This book includes dishes made with nuts and
   nut derivatives. It is advisable for customers with
   known allergic reactions to nuts and nut
   derivatives and those who may be potentially
   vulnerable to these allergies, such as pregnant
   and nursing mothers, invalids, the elderly,
   babies, and children, to avoid dishes made with
   nuts and nut oils. it is also prudent to check the
   lables of preprepared ingredients for the possible
   inclusion of nut dervatives.
8. Vegetarians should look for special labeling on
   cheese to ensure that it is made with vegetarian
   rennet. There are vegetarian forms of Parmesan,
   feta, cheddar, Cheshire, Red Leicester, dolcelatte
   and many goat cheeses, among others.

Contents

Introduction

Cooking for me started at a very young age when I would help my mom in the kitchen (I'm not sure if it was help but it was always great fun), spilling sugar and flour everywhere and seeing who could mix the fastest! As soon as she taught me that part of cooking was also cleaning up, I was allowed to cook more and more: cakes on Saturday afternoon then; later, fish pies and lasagna. I went to a boarding school with dreadful food, but on Tuesdays it was domestic science; I would try to make a decent meal for a few friends to enjoy. Everyone relied on it working out, which it generally did.

I think that these early days played a great part in creating the foundations for my cooking career. I still enjoy it and continue to learn: it's a never-ending creative process of combining colors, flavors, and textures to produce a delicious meal to enjoy with friends.

I have aimed to produce imaginative and tasty recipes that are quick and simple to make (and good for you, too). The recipes in this book have been designed to show that it is possible to produce delicious, mouth-watering meals in 30 minutes—the same length of time that it takes to heat up many ready-made meals—or even less time, without resorting to convenience food.

Italian recipes fit the bill perfectly when you need good quick meals in a hurry, as the Italians are very insistent on fresh food and speedy methods of preparation. They take their food very seriously, combining a deep respect for top-quality ingredients with a great love of home cooking—in fact, the way to enjoy Italian food at its best is to eat in people's homes.

Italian food, in all its rich, regional diversity, doesn't just taste delicious, it's actually good for you, too. The Mediterranean diet, with its emphasis on fresh vegetables and fruit, fresh fish and seafood, pasta and olive oil, is believed to be one of the healthiest in the world, full of vitamins and minerals and low in saturated fat.

In this book I have included a lot of vegetables that work very well as supper dishes on their own. Serve two or three vegetable, pasta, or rice dishes together, enjoy their delicate flavors, and see how satisfied you feel after the meal without feeling at all heavy or as if you have eaten too much. There are some delicious meat and fish recipes, too, that can be cooked in 30 minutes; a joy to

any busy cook who doesn't want to be chained to the stove when the sun is shining outside or after a busy day at work or with the children. There are also some desserts for special days.
I have to say that I am especially proud of the chocolate risotto, which is a totally new idea and is easy to make from ingredients that will be found in any well-stocked kitchen.

Follow the Italian example and shop carefully, though. Some of the cheaper products in our shops and supermarkets are very poor substitutes for the real thing. Never, for example, buy ready-grated Parmesan. Instead, buy a piece and grate it as required. A guide to the most important or unusual ingredients used in the recipes appears in the glossary that follows.

Ivan Warde.

Glossary

Balsamic vinegar

This aristocrat of vinegars is made in Modena. The grape juice is aged in wooden barrels for an average of seven years. Like a good wine, it needs time to mature, and the longer it is in the barrel the deeper and sweeter the flavor—and the higher the price.

Capers

Used to flavor sauces, these are the pungent, sharp-tasting buds of a shrub found in Mediterranean countries. Capers are usually bottled in brine and need to be rinsed in water before using. Small ones are the best.

Cavolo nero

A long, slim cabbage with a distinct sweet flavor; it is a beautiful green with a hint of purplish black.

Chocolate

Bars of chocolate vary so much in their cocoa content. Look on the back of the package and only use ones that contain at least 70% cocoa solids. I prefer Valrhona, which can be found in good delicatessens.

Cheeses

Dolcelatte A soft creamy cow's milk cheese with blue veins, aged for 2 months; it is similar to Gorgonzola but milder.

Fontina A soft cow's milk cheese from the Val d'Aosta in the Italian Alps, that is aged for up to five months. It is reminiscent of Gruyère and used in cooking and as a dessert cheese.

Mascarpone A soft creamy cheese made with cow's milk and used for sweet and savory dishes.

Mozzarella Originally made from buffalo's milk, it is now more often made from cow's milk or a mixture of the two. cow's milk mozzarella does not have the same softness of flavor. Mozzarella should be eaten fresh; it melts well and is frequently used on pizzas.

Parmesan This strong, hard cheese is made from partially skimmed cow's milk and aged for up to two years. The best Parmesan has the words *Parmigiano-Reggiano* punched into the rind. Buy it in a block and grate it as you need it.

Pecorino This sheep's milk cheese can be soft or hard depending on its age; it is made all over Italy so flavors can vary greatly. Mature, hard pecorino is used for grating like Parmesan.

Ricotta A bland, soft, fresh cheese used as a base in fillings and frequently combined with spinach. It should be used when it is very fresh.

Ciabatta

A popular Italian bread baked into a flat loaf with a distinctive open texture. It can have a range of flavorings added.

Fennel

A beautiful fragrant vegetable with a delicate aniseed flavor, fennel is wonderful with fish; use the feathery fronds to add to salsa verde.

Focaccia

A flat yeast bread made with olive oil and baked in an oiled pan. It is often flavored with garlic, herbs, sun-dried tomatoes, or olives.

Garlic
A pungent herb used extensively in Italian cooking. Crush heavily with the side of a knife to remove the papery skin; then the clove can be chopped.

Herbs
Basil The best-known Italian herb, with soft, bright-green leaves, basil is a vital ingredient in pesto and goes well with tomatoes. There is also a red basil with small, purplish leaves and a more delicate flavor.
Bay leaves Usually used dried in soups and stews as part of a bouquet garni.
Oregano A sweet, spicy, and aromatic herb, similar to marjoram.
Rosemary Its long, spiky leaves give rosemary a distinctive appearance. It is used a great deal in Italy, particularly with chicken and lamb. It is very pungent, so should be used in moderation.

Olive oil
Extra virgin olive oil, virgin olive oil, and olive oil. These names refer to the way that the oil is extracted and this can greatly alter the flavor. Try to buy extra virgin oil from the first cold pressing, as this will be rich in flavor and is most suitable for dressings, sauces, and pouring over pasta. A less expensive oil can be used for frying.

Olives
Small, oval tree fruits that ripen from green to black. For the best flavor, buy them from delicatessens that sell them loose rather than in bottles or cans.

Pancetta
The same cut as bacon but differently cured, pancetta is found in supermarkets or in delicatessens. It is also sold as pancetta arrotolata, in a roll like salami. Buy a ½-inch slice, unroll it, and use as pancetta.

Panettone
A baked yeast cake from Milan enriched with egg yolks, raisins, and candied peel. Panettone is traditionally served at Christmas or with coffee; it is very good toasted at breakfast.

Parma ham
A great Italian delicacy, this cured ham comes from the area around Parma in the Emilia-Romagna region of northern Italy. The skin is rubbed in salt, then the hams are hung in cellars to mature for 8–10 months. Parma ham must be served thinly sliced; it is eaten on its own or with melon or figs.

Pasta
This is made from hard durum wheat flour and water. If it is made with eggs, it is called pasta all'ouvo. I prefer fresh pasta, but a good dried Italian brand can be substituted. The Italians do not usually eat pasta as a main course, but serve a light pasta dish between the antipasti and the main course. It is available in a bewildering range of shapes and sizes.

Pasta shapes
Farfalle or farfallini Pasta bows.
Fusilli Pasta twists or corkscrews.
Lasagna Large sheets of pasta used for baked dishes. Sheets can be cut to fit cooking dishes.
Linguine Long, thin, flat ribbon noodles.
Pappardelle Wide pasta noodles.
Penne Sometimes known as quills, these are a short, tubular lengths of pasta.
Orecchiette Small, round ear-shaped pasta.
Orzo A very small pasta shape, that looks rather like grains of rice.
Spaghetti Long, string-like pasta.
Tagliatelle Long, flat ribbon noodles.
Tortellini Pasta twists with various fillings.

Pine nuts
Small, slim, soft nuts with an oily texture, these come from the Mediterranean stone pine tree. Pine nuts, also known as pine kernels, are used in pasta sauces, stuffings, and salads and are usually browned before using. They turn rancid quickly, so store them in a refrigerator.

Polenta Ground corn kernels mixed with water, made into a flat golden loaf, sliced, and broiled. Polenta needs to be flavored as it is bland, although it is rich in vitamins. It can also be served in a softer form, like mashed potatoes.

Pumpkin seed oil Pressed from roasted pumpkin seeds, this thick, brown oil, tinged with green, has a powerful, toasted flavor.

Puy lentils Small, round lentils, greenish brown in color and far superior to any other lentil for texture and flavor. They come from the area around Le Puy in France.

Risotto rice Arborio is the classic risotto rice from Piedmont. It absorbs a lot of cooking liquid without becoming too soft. The grain is plump and irregular, translucent at the edges with a hard, white core. It produces a creamy risotto with a slight bite. Carnaroli is very similar.

Saffron The dried stigmas of a species of crocus, with a pungent aroma, bitter flavor, and a beautiful golden color. Buy it in Spain or at duty-free shops where it is cheaper and comes in larger containers.

Sea salt I think Maldon sea salt from Essex is by far the best; there are no additives and the large, flaky crystals are fantastic on a salad or used at the table.

Squash These are members of the marrow and pumpkin family; the best is butternut squash for its sweet flavor and dense texture.

Sun-dried tomatoes Intensely flavored dried tomatoes that add zip to a dish. Those bottled in oil are more convenient to use than the dried variety, which need to be soaked before use.

Truffle oil The infusion of truffle juices into an oil, usually extra virgin olive oil. White truffle oil is usually more expensive and stronger in flavor than black truffle oil. Use both sparingly as they have an intense flavor.

Wild mushrooms

Chanterelles Wonderful aromatic mushrooms with a perfumed taste, chanterelles are shaped like open horns, torn around the edges. They vary in color from brown to gold and dry well.

Morels Mushrooms with bulbous pitted caps and an intense aroma. Fresh morels need to be cleaned well. They are also found dried and bottled.

Porcini Delicious mushrooms with a deep, rich flavor, porcini have a round, bun-like cap, a thick chubby stalk, and fleshy texture. They are sold fresh and dried. Soak dried porcinì in hot water for 15 minutes before use, then drain, filter, and reserve the water to use as a rich stock.

Truffles The mysterious king of fungi, these are found below ground near oak trees and are sniffed out by pigs or dogs in autumn and winter. Usually the size of a walnut, truffles are rough on the outside, dense inside, and firm to the touch. Both white and black truffles are found; their flavor is so intense that only a little is needed. Truffles are best served raw, finely shaved over salad or pasta.

Soups

In Italy soup is served as a *primo piatto*, first course, as an alternative to rice or pasta. Many of the soups are hearty, based on beans, vegetables, and bread, and thus make complete meals in themselves.

Preparation time **10 minutes**   Cooking time **20 minutes**
Total time **30 minutes**   *Serves 4*

spinach and broccoli soup

one   Heat the oil and butter in a saucepan, add the onion and garlic, and sauté for 3 minutes.

two   Add the chopped potatoes, broccoli, spinach, and stock, bring to a boil, and simmer for 15 minutes.

three   This soup can be puréed or left with chunky pieces. Add the Gorgonzola to the soup with the lemon juice, nutmeg, and salt and pepper to taste. Garnish with the toasted pine nuts and serve with warm crusty bread.

2 tablespoons olive oil
4 tablespoons butter
1 onion, diced
1 garlic clove, crushed and chopped
2 potatoes, chopped
8 oz. broccoli, chopped
10 oz. spinach, washed and chopped
3 cups chicken or vegetable stock
4 oz. Gorgonzola cheese, crumbled into
    small pieces
juice of ½ lemon
½ teaspoon grated nutmeg
salt and pepper
3 oz. toasted pine nuts, to garnish

Preparation time **10 minutes**   Total time **10 minutes**   *Serves 4*

melon and Parma ham soup

1 ripe cantaloupe or charentais melon, weighing about 3 lbs.
8 slices Parma ham
salt and pepper
red basil leaves, torn, to garnish

one   Cut the melon in half and remove the seeds. Scoop the flesh into a food processor and process until smooth; then add salt and pepper to taste.

two   Finely dice 4 of the ham slices and stir them into the soup. Cut the remaining 4 slices into thin ribbons.

three   Garnish the soup with the ham ribbons and torn basil leaves.

Serve at room temperature or just slightly chilled.
When food is too cold you cannot taste its full flavor.

Preparation time **10 minutes**
Cooking time **20 minutes**
Total time **30 minutes**   *Serves 4*

pesto and green vegetable soup

Pesto:
3 garlic cloves, crushed and chopped
handful of basil leaves
2 tablespoons pine nuts
2 oz. Parmesan cheese, freshly grated
3 tablespoons olive oil

Soup:
3 tablespoons olive oil
1 onion, diced
2 leeks, sliced
1 potato, chopped
14 oz. can navy beans, drained and rinsed
6¼ cups vegetable stock
2 zucchini, diced
4 oz. small green beans, cut into small pieces
4 oz. broccoli florets, chopped
8 oz. canned artichoke hearts
1 tablespoon flat-leafed parsley, chopped
salt and pepper

one   To make the pesto, put the garlic, basil, pine nuts, and Parmesan in a food processor or blender and purée thoroughly. Add the oil and blend again. Set aside.

two   Heat the oil for the soup in a saucepan, add the onion and leeks, and cook over gentle heat for about 3 minutes.

three   Add the potato, navy beans, stock, and salt and pepper to taste, bring to a boil and simmer for 12 minutes.

four   Add the zucchini, green beans, broccoli, and artichoke hearts and simmer for 5 minutes.

five   Finally, add the chopped parsley and pesto and stir well. Serve immediately with warm focaccia bread.

Preparation time **5 minutes**
Cooking time **25 minutes**
Total time **30 minutes**
Serves 4

zucchini soup

This soup is delicious served cold in the summer, as the lemon gives it a really fresh, clean taste.

2 tablespoons olive oil
4 shallots, diced
1 garlic clove, crushed and chopped
6 zucchini, diced
2 potatoes, chopped
4 cups chicken stock
3 oz. farfallini or other small pasta
juice and rind of 1 lemon
large handful of chives, chopped
salt and pepper

one   Heat the oil in a saucepan, add the shallots and garlic, and sauté gently for 3 minutes.

two   Add the zucchini, potatoes, and stock, simmer for 15 minutes, then pass through a sieve or whirl in a blender until smooth.

three   Add the pasta and cook for about 7 minutes until soft.

four   Stir in the lemon rind, juice, and chives. Season with salt and pepper and serve at once.

Preparation time **5 minutes**   Cooking time **25 minutes**   Total time **30 minutes**   *Serves 4*

butternut squash soup

1 butternut squash, weighing 1¾ lb.
4 tablespoons butter
2 tablespoons olive oil
2 onions, chopped
1 garlic clove, crushed and chopped
4 cups chicken or vegetable stock
pinch of saffron threads
salt and pepper
To serve:
2 rosemary sprigs, chopped
3 oz. Parmesan cheese, freshly grated

one   To prepare the squash, cut it in half and remove all the seeds, peel off the skin, and chop the flesh into small cubes.

two   Heat the butter and oil in a saucepan, add the onion, garlic, and squash, and sauté for 5 minutes.

three   Add the stock and saffron, bring to a boil, and simmer for 15 minutes.

four   Pour the soup into a food processor and purée. Season generously with salt and pepper.

five   To serve, ladle into warmed bowls and sprinkle each one with chopped rosemary and a generous spoonful of grated Parmesan.

Preparation time **5 minutes**
Cooking time **25 minutes**
Total time **30 minutes**   *Serves 4*

minestrone soup

Minestrone improves when it is made in advance and reheated. Cover and store in the refrigerator so that the flavors can blend.

2 tablespoons olive oil
1 onion, diced
1 garlic clove, crushed and chopped
2 celery stalks, chopped
1 leek, finely sliced
1 carrot, chopped
13 oz. can chopped tomatoes
2½ cups chicken or vegetable stock
1 zucchini, diced
½ small cabbage, shredded
1 bay leaf
3 oz. canned navy beans
3 oz. spaghetti, broken into small pieces
1 tablespoon chopped flat-leafed parsley
salt and pepper
To serve:
2 oz. Parmesan cheese, freshly grated
Bruschetta (see page 20)

one   Heat the oil in a saucepan, add the onion, garlic, celery, leek, and carrot and sauté for 3 minutes.

two   Add the tomatoes, stock, zucchini, cabbage, bay leaf, and navy beans. Bring to a boil and simmer for 10 minutes.

three   Add the broken spaghetti and season with salt and pepper to taste. Stir well and cook for a further 8 minutes. Keep stirring, as the soup may stick to the bottom of the pan.

four   Just before serving add the chopped parsley and stir well. Serve with grated Parmesan and bruschetta.

Like Minestrone, Tuscan bean soup can be reheated and, as it improves with keeping, it is really worth making the day before and storing in the refrigerator, allowing all the flavors to mingle.

Preparation time **5 minutes**   Cooking time **25 minutes**   Total time **30 minutes**   *Serves 4*

Tuscan bean soup

2 tablespoons olive oil
4 shallots, chopped
2 garlic cloves, crushed and chopped
5 oz. piece of bacon, diced
1 carrot, diced
2 celery stalks, diced
½ red pepper, cored, deseeded, and diced
14 oz. can borlotti beans, drained and rinsed
4 cups chicken stock
1 bay leaf
1 teaspoon chopped oregano
1 teaspoon chopped marjoram
handful of flat-leafed parsley, chopped
salt and pepper
extra virgin olive oil, to drizzle

one   Heat the oil in a saucepan, add the shallots, garlic, bacon, carrot, celery, and red pepper, and cook, stirring occasionally, for 5 minutes.

two   Add the beans, stock, bay leaf, oregano, and marjoram, bring to a boil and simmer for 15 minutes. Skim off any scum that may come from the beans.

three   Taste and season well. Finally, just before serving, add the chopped parsley.

four   To serve, ladle into warmed bowls and drizzle each one with a little extra virgin olive oil.

Preparation time **10 minutes**   Cooking time **10 minutes**   Total time **20 minutes**   *Serves 4*

mussel soup

one   Warm the olive oil in a large saucepan. Add the onions, garlic, chili, and bacon, and sauté for 5 minutes.

two   Check the mussels carefully. Discard any that are open or do not close immediately when tapped on a work surface.

three   Add the mussels, tomatoes, wine, saffron, and season with salt and pepper; mix well. Place a tight-fitting lid on the pan and simmer for 5 minutes, or until all the mussel shells have opened. Discard any mussels with shells that remain shut.

four   Add the parsley, stir well, and serve at once.

2 tablespoons olive oil
2 onions, chopped
2 garlic cloves, crushed and chopped
1 red chili, chopped
5 oz. piece of bacon, chopped
2 lb. mussels, scrubbed and debearded
13 oz. can chopped tomatoes
½ bottle dry white wine
good pinch of saffron threads
handful of flat-leafed parsley, roughly chopped
salt and pepper

Preparation time **5 minutes**   Cooking time **5 minutes**
Total time **10 minutes**   *Serves 4*

bruschetta

8 slices ciabatta bread
2 garlic cloves, peeled
small handful of flat-leafed
parsley, chopped
5 tablespoons olive oil
salt

Bruschetta is delicious served with many different Italian dishes, especially soup and fish. It is a very useful accompaniment as the bread does not have to be fresh.

one   Toast the bread under a preheated broiler until golden brown.

two   Rub the garlic over one side of the bread; the bread acts as a grater and the garlic is evenly spread over the bread. Sprinkle the bruschetta with the parsley and salt and drizzle with olive oil. Serve immediately or keep warm until required, but do not keep warm for too long or the bruschetta will lose its crunchiness.

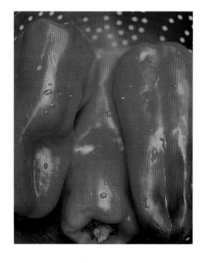

Preparation time **10 minutes**
Cooking time **5 minutes**
Total time **15 minutes**
Serves 4

crostini

one   Toast the bread under a preheated broiler until golden brown.

two   Rub the garlic over the bread on one side; the bread acts as a grater and the garlic is evenly spread over the bread. Sprinkle with parsley and salt and drizzle with olive oil.

three   Mix together the red peppers, olives, and crumbled goat cheese, and season with pepper.

four   Spread the mixture evenly over the toasted bruschetta and place under a preheated low broiler for 2 minutes to just melt the cheese. Serve at once.

Variation: Sliced tomatoes, sprinkled with oregano and pepper, are also very good on bruschetta.

8 slices ciabatta bread
2 garlic cloves, peeled
small handful of flat-leafed parsley,
chopped
5 tablespoons olive oil
1–2 red peppers, peeled and sliced
into strips
3 oz. black olives, pitted
4 oz. goat cheese, crumbled
salt and pepper

Crostini are an extension of bruschetta; the base is the same, but the crostini have many different toppings. They are great with soup; if you want to serve a simple supper there is nothing better than a good homemade soup, crostini with your favorite topping, and a fresh green salad.

Pasta

More than 200 different shapes of pasta are available in Italy, and every region has its own particular specialties and ways of serving them. Pasta is one of the most versatile Italian foods and may be baked, stuffed, and tossed in sauces or dressings.

Preparation time **10 minutes**   Cooking time **10 minutes**   Total time **20 minutes**   *Serves 4*

linguine with vegetables

1 red pepper, cored, deseeded,
and cut in to large squares
1 zucchini, sliced
1 red onion, sliced
1 small eggplant, sliced into
thin rounds
8 asparagus spears, trimmed
5 tablespoons olive oil
10 oz. linguine
3 tablespoons frozen tiny new
green peas
4 oz. Parmesan cheese,
freshly grated
handful of basil leaves,
roughly torn
salt and pepper

one   The vegetables can be cooked either on a griddle or broiled. To cook them on a griddle, heat the griddle, then add the peppers, skin side down, and cook until the skin blisters and blackens. Cook the zucchini, onion, and eggplant slices and the asparagus for 2 minutes on each side. Alternatively, cook all the vegetables under a preheated hot broiler.

two   Place a large saucepan of water on to boil for the pasta.

three   Peel the skin off the pepper and slice into ribbons. Place in a dish with the zucchini, onion, eggplant, and asparagus, drizzle with olive oil, and put into a warm oven to keep warm.

four   Place the pasta in the boiling water and cook for 3–4 minutes if fresh and 8 minutes if dried, or according to package instructions. Test a piece before draining. Add the peas for the last minute of the cooking time.

five   Drain the pasta and peas in a colander, then return to the saucepan. Add the warm vegetables, season with salt and pepper, and add the Parmesan. Toss well, using two spoons, adding a little more olive oil if necessary. Finally, add the torn basil leaves and toss again, then serve immediately.

Preparation time **15 minutes**   Cooking time **15 minutes**
Total time **30 minutes**   *Serves 4*

pasta primavera

2 tablespoons olive oil
1 garlic clove, crushed and chopped
2 shallots, chopped
4 oz. shelled peas
4 oz. young fava beans, shelled and gray skins
removed
4 oz. asparagus, trimmed and cut into lengths
4 oz. spinach, washed and chopped
10 oz. tagliatelle
½ cup whipping cream
3 oz. Parmesan cheese,
freshly grated
handful of mint leaves, chopped
salt and pepper

one   Place a large saucepan of water on to boil for the tagliatelle.

two   Heat the oil in a saucepan, add the garlic and shallots, and sauté for 3 minutes. Add the peas, fava beans, asparagus, and spinach to the shallot mixture. Stir well and cook for 2 minutes.

three   Put the tagliatelle into the boiling water and cook for 3 minutes if fresh and 7 minutes if dried, or according to package instructions. Stir the pasta while it is cooking.

four   Stir the cream into the vegetables, mix well, and simmer for 3 minutes.

five   Drain the tagliatelle thoroughly, then add the pasta to the vegetable sauce and season well with salt and pepper. Add the Parmesan and mint and toss thoroughly with two spoons. Serve at once.

Cook the vegetables for this dish on a heated griddle pan or under a preheated hot broiler; this intensifies the flavors of the vegetables.

Preparation time **5 minutes**　Cooking time **10 minutes**
Total time **15 minutes**　*Serves 4*

saffron bows

10 oz. farfalle
2 tablespoons butter
½ cup heavy cream
½ teaspoon saffron threads
salt and pepper
3 oz. Parmesan cheese,
freshly grated, to serve

one　Place a large saucepan of water on to boil for the pasta. When it is boiling, add the pasta and stir well. Cook for 3 minutes if fresh and 6 minutes if dried, or according to package instructions.

two　Heat the butter and cream in a small saucepan, add the saffron, and gently bring to a simmer; the yellow of the saffron will explode into the cream and a fantastic subtle aroma will fill the kitchen.

three　Drain the pasta well, place in a warmed serving bowl, and pour the saffron sauce over. Season with salt and pepper and mix well.

four　Serve the Parmesan at the table and sprinkle just a little over each portion.

Saffron threads are the dried stigmas of a species of crocus. Saffron is a costly spice, but a little is all you need to transform a dish.

Preparation time **10 minutes**
Cooking time **20 minutes**
Total time **30 minutes**
Serves 4

penne with tomato and chili

one　Heat the oil in a saucepan, add the onion and garlic, and sauté until soft; do not let them brown. Add the chilies.

two　Place a large saucepan of water on to boil for the penne. When the water is boiling, add the penne and cook for 6 minutes if fresh and 10 minutes if dried, or according to package instructions.

three　Cut a cross at the stem end of each tomato. Place the tomatoes in a bowl and pour boiling water over to cover. Let stand for 1–2 minutes, then drain and peel off the skins. Cut the tomatoes into quarters, remove the seeds, and cut lengthwise into strips.

four　Add the tomatoes to the onion mixture. Over low heat, add the sugar, vinegar, and salt and pepper. Mix gently and simmer slowly until the pasta is cooked.

five　Drain the pasta well. Stir the parsley into the tomato sauce. Add the sauce to the pasta, mix well, adding a dash of extra virgin olive oil, if desired. Serve with a bowl of grated Parmesan.

3 tablespoons olive oil
1 onion, chopped
2 garlic cloves, crushed and chopped
2 pinches crushed dried chilies, or to taste
10 oz. penne pasta
10 plum tomatoes
1 teaspoon sugar
1 teaspoon vinegar
handful of flat-leafed parsley, chopped
extra virgin olive oil, optional
salt and pepper
3 oz. Parmesan cheese, freshly grated, to serve

Preparation time **5 minutes**   Cooking time **15 minutes**   Total time **20 minutes**   *Serves 4*

fusilli with Parmesan and pine nuts

10 oz. fusilli
4 oz. pine nuts
6 tablespoons butter
2 tablespoons olive oil
3 oz. Parmesan cheese,
freshly grated
handful of basil leaves
salt and pepper

one   Place a large saucepan of water on to boil for the pasta. Put the fusilli into the boiling water and cook for 3–4 minutes if fresh, for 7 minutes if dried, or according to package instructions. Test before draining.

two   Toast the pine nuts under the broiler or in a pan over moderate heat. Watch them all the time and move them around to brown evenly.

three   Melt the butter with the oil in a small saucepan. Drain the pasta well, pour the butter over, season with salt and pepper, and toss well.

four   Turn into a warmed serving dish, sprinkle with the pine nuts, Parmesan, and basil leaves, and serve immediately.

Preparation time **10 minutes**
Cooking time **15 minutes**
Total time **25 minutes**   *Serves 4*

pappardelle with olives and capers

4 oz. black or green olives, pitted
2 pinches crushed dried chilies
2 tablespoons capers, chopped
7 anchovy fillets, drained and chopped
4 large pieces sun-dried tomatoes soaked in olive oil
10 oz. pappardelle
large handful of parsley, chopped
3 oz. Parmesan cheese, freshly grated
salt and pepper

one   Place a large saucepan of water on to boil for the pappardelle.

two   Coarsely chop the olives. Put them into a saucepan with the chilies, capers, and anchovies. Chop the sun-dried tomatoes coarsely and add them to the saucepan with 4 tablespoons of the olive oil.

three   Put the pasta into the boiling water and cook for 4 minutes if fresh and 7 minutes if dried, or according to package instructions. Test a piece before draining.

four   Gently heat the olive mixture for 4 minutes until warm; do not let it fry.

five   Drain the pasta, add the warmed olive mixture, parsley, and Parmesan. Season with salt and pepper. Mix well with two spoons and serve. This dish can also be allowed to stand for a while and served at room temperature.

Preparation time **5 minutes**
Cooking time **10 minutes**
Total time **15 minutes**   *Serves 4*

spinach tortellini with blue cheese dressing

1 lb. spinach tortellini
10 oz. Gorgonzola or dolcelatte cheese
6 tablespoons butter
½ cup heavy cream
pepper

one   Place a large saucepan of water on to boil for the tortellini. Put the pasta into the boiling water and cook for 5 minutes if fresh and 8–9 if dried, or according to package instructions. Remove a piece and test, before draining.

two   Crumble the cheese into a small saucepan, add the butter and cream, and place over low heat to melt the cheese and warm the mixture.

three   Drain the pasta well, add the warm cheese sauce, toss well, and serve immediately. This is delicious and very rich; a crisp, lightly dressed salad is a good accompaniment.

Preparation time **10 minutes**
Cooking time **10 minutes**
Total time **20 minutes**   *Serves 4*

lemon and basil orzo

one   Place a large saucepan of water on to boil for the orzo.

two   Using a mortar and pestle or a food processor, blend the garlic, basil, olive oil, lemon rind, and juice until smooth.

three   Place the orzo in the boiling water and cook for 6–8 minutes, or according to package instructions.

four   Add the Parmesan to the basil mixture, blend well, and season with salt and pepper.

five   Drain the orzo thoroughly. Add the pesto and mix well so that the sauce is distributed evenly throughout the orzo. Serve immediately.

2 garlic cloves, crushed and chopped
large handful of basil leaves
5 tablespoons olive oil
rind and juice of 2 lemons
10 oz. dried orzo
5 oz. Parmesan cheese, freshly grated
salt and pepper

Preparation time **10 minutes**   Cooking time **18 minutes**   Total time **28 minutes**   *Serves 4*

penne with fava beans, asparagus, and mint

1 lb. asparagus, trimmed and cut into 2-inch lengths
4 tablespoons olive oil
8 oz. fava beans or peas
10 oz. penne
¼ cup plus 2 tablespoons heavy cream
3 oz. Parmesan cheese, freshly grated
4 tablespoons chopped mint
salt and pepper

one   Place a large saucepan of water on to boil for the pasta.

two   Place the asparagus on a baking sheet, brush generously with olive oil, and season with salt and pepper. Place under a preheated broiler and cook for 8 minutes, turning as they brown.

three   Meanwhile, cook the fava beans or peas in lightly salted boiling water for 2 minutes.

four   Put the pasta in the boiling water and cook for 6 minutes if fresh and 10 minutes if dried, or according to package instructions. Remove a piece and test before draining.

five   Pour the cream into the empty pasta pan over the heat, add the cooked fava beans or peas, broiled asparagus, Parmesan, and season with salt and pepper. Return the pasta to the pan, add the mint, and toss well with two wooden spoons. Serve at once.

This dish is delicious and very good in the summer because of the fresh taste of the lemon and basil. If orzo is not available, another pasta shape can be substituted.

Preparation time **10 minutes**   Cooking time **20 minutes**   Total time **30 minutes**   *Serves 4*

mushroom and mozzarella lasagna stacks

2 tablespoons olive oil
4 tablespoons butter
2 onions, chopped
2 garlic cloves, crushed and chopped
1 lb. mushrooms, sliced
4 tablespoons heavy cream
4 tablespoons dry white wine
1 teaspoon chopped thyme
8 pieces fresh lasagna
2 red peppers, cored, deseeded, skinned, and thickly sliced
4 oz. package buffalo mozzarella cheese, sliced
4 oz. baby spinach leaves, washed and trimmed
2 oz. Parmesan cheese
salt and pepper

one   Heat the oil and butter in a saucepan, add the onions, and sauté for 3 minutes. Add the garlic and cook for 1 minute.

two   Add the mushrooms, turn up the heat, and cook for 5 minutes.

three   Add the cream, white wine, and thyme; season with salt and pepper and simmer for 4 minutes.

four   Bring a pan of water to a boil; add the lasagna, a few pieces at a time, checking that it does not stick together, and cook for 3 minutes if fresh or 7 minutes if dried. Remove from the pan and place 4 pieces in a well-oiled large ovenproof dish.

five   Place a generous spoonful of mushroom mixture on each piece of lasagna, add some red pepper slices and half of the spinach leaves, and put another piece of lasagna on top. Then add the remaining spinach leaves, a slice of mozzarella, and top with a little more mushroom mixture. Finish with some Parmesan shavings. Place the lasagna portions under a preheated very hot broiler and cook for 5 minutes until the mushroom mixture is bubbling and the Parmesan is golden.

Preparation time **10 minutes**   Cooking time **10 minutes**
Total time **20 minutes**   *Serves 4*

tagliatelle with fresh truffles

Truffles are in season in the autumn and early winter months, and you can find them in specialty delicatessens. They are very expensive but a great treat. It really isn't worth using truffles from a can or jar as they bear no resemblance to the flavor of fresh truffles.

10 oz. dried tagliatelle
4 oz. truffles
8 tablespoons butter
½ tablespoon truffle oil
handful of flat-leafed parsley, chopped
3 oz. Parmesan cheese, freshly grated
salt and pepper

one   Place a large saucepan of water on to boil for the tagliatelle. Put the pasta into the boiling water and cook for 8 minutes, or according to package instructions, stirring from time to time.

two   While the pasta is cooking, clean the truffles with a clean dry soft brush, dusting away any dirt. Finely slice the truffles using a mandoline.

three   Drain the pasta, add the butter, truffle oil, parsley, Parmesan, and season with salt and pepper to taste and toss well.

four   Add half of the sliced truffles to the pasta and toss again. Serve garnished with the remaining truffles.

This dish can be cooked in advance except for the final browning of the Parmesan. Reheat in a moderate oven for 20 minutes, then broil until golden.

Preparation time **10 minutes**   Cooking time **20 minutes**   Total time **30 minutes**   *Serves 4*

spaghetti vongole with flat-leafed parsley

3 lbs. baby clams (vongole)
4 tablespoons olive oil
2 garlic cloves, crushed and chopped
½ cup dry white wine
¼ cup plus 2 tablespoons heavy cream
1 lb. spaghetti
large handful of flat-leafed parsley, chopped
salt and pepper
freshly grated Parmesan cheese, to serve

one   To wash the vongole, place them in a colander and submerge in a bowl of cold water. Shake vigorously, then lift out the colander and replace with fresh water. Repeat until the vongole are clean, then drain well. Check the vongole and discard any that are damaged or open.

two   Heat the oil in a large saucepan over low heat, add the garlic and vongole, cover, and cook for 3 minutes or until all the vongole have opened. Discard any that do not open.

three   Lift the vongole out of the pan with a slotted spoon. Remove half of them from their shells and return any liquid to the pan. Set the vongole aside.

four   Add the wine and cream to the pan and increase the heat to reduce the sauce.

five   Meanwhile, bring a large pan of boiling water to a boil, add the spaghetti, and cook for 3–4 minutes if fresh, 8 minutes if dried, or according to package instructions, until just tender. Check a piece before draining.

six   Return the vongole to the sauce, stir well, and simmer for 2 minutes. Add the parsley and spaghetti to the vongole, season with salt and pepper, and mix well, using two spoons to combine the spaghetti with the sauce.

seven   Serve immediately with freshly grated Parmesan.

Preparation time **5 minutes**   Cooking time **15 minutes**
Total time **20 minutes**   *Serves 4*

tagliatelle with crab sauce

one   Heat the olive oil in a saucepan, add the shallots, and sauté gently until soft, but do not brown.

two   Add the crab meat, chilies, lemon rind, and juice, and season with salt and pepper.

three   Place a large saucepan of water on to boil for the tagliatelle. When it is boiling, add the tagliatelle and cook for 3–4 minutes if fresh, 6 minutes if dried, or according to package instructions. Test a piece before draining.

four   Add the cream to the crab mixture and bring to a boil.

five   Drain the tagliatelle well. Add the chives to the crab mixture.

six   Add the sauce to the tagliatelle; mix well, and serve with a bowl of grated Parmesan.

2 tablespoons olive oil
2 shallots, chopped
7 oz. crab meat
1–2 pinches dried chili, crumbled
grated rind and juice of 1 lemon
10 oz. tagliatelle
4 tablespoons heavy cream
handful of chives, snipped
salt and pepper
3 oz. Parmesan cheese, freshly grated, to serve

spaghetti with lobster

2 lb. cooked lobster, cut in half lengthwise
4 tablespoons olive oil
2 shallots, chopped
8 plum tomatoes, skinned, deseeded, and chopped
juice of 1 lemon
10 oz. spaghetti
handful of chives, chopped
salt and pepper

one   Place a large saucepan of water on to boil for the spaghetti.

two   Remove all the meat from the lobster and cut it into chunks.

three   Heat the oil in a saucepan, add the shallots, and sauté for 3 minutes. Add the tomatoes and lemon juice, season with salt and pepper, and cook for a further 3 minutes.

four   Place the spaghetti in the boiling water, stir, and cook for 3–4 minutes if fresh or 8 minutes if dried, or according to package instructions.

five   Add the lobster to the tomato sauce, stir, reduce the heat, and cook for 4 minutes.

six   Drain the pasta well. Add the sauce to the pasta with the chopped chives, toss with two wooden spoons, and serve immediately.

This dish makes an excellent quick meal to serve to friends—the addition of lobster makes it really special.

Preparation time **10 minutes**   Cooking time **15 minutes**
Total time **25 minutes**   *Serves 4*

pappardelle with prosciutto and porcini

Fresh or dried porcini may be used for this recipe. If you use dried porcini, use 4 oz. and soak them in hot water for 15 minutes to rehydrate.

2 tablespoons olive oil
1 garlic clove, crushed and chopped
8 oz. porcini, sliced
8 oz. prosciutto
10 oz. pappardelle
½ cup whipping cream
handful of flat-leafed parsley, chopped
3 oz. Parmesan cheese,
freshly grated
salt and pepper

one   Place a large saucepan of water on to boil for the pappardelle.

two   Heat the olive oil in a saucepan, add the garlic and porcini, and sauté for 4 minutes over moderate heat.

three   Cut the prosciutto into strips; try to keep them separate.

four   Place the pappardelle in the boiling water and cook for 4 minutes if fresh and 9 minutes if dried, or according to package instructions. Test a piece before draining.

five   Add the prosciutto, cream, and parsley to the porcini and season with salt and pepper. Bring to a boil and simmer for 1 minute.

six   Add the pappardelle to the sauce and toss well, using two spoons to mix evenly. Sprinkle with the Parmesan, toss well, and serve at once.

Preparation time **10 minutes**
Cooking time **15 minutes**
Total time **25 minutes**   *Serves 4*

spaghetti carbonara

The true Italian way to serve spaghetti carbonara is with an egg yolk in its shell on top of each serving, which is mixed in by the person eating.

one   Heat the oil in a saucepan, add the bacon, and cook gently for 3 minutes. Add the garlic and cook for 1 minute.

two   Place a large saucepan of water on to boil for the spaghetti. When it is boiling, add the spaghetti and cook for 3–4 minutes if fresh, or 8 minutes if dried, or according to package instructions. Remove a piece and test. Drain when cooked and return to the pan.

three   Beat the cream and egg yolks together, add to the bacon, and mix well over low heat.

four   Add the sauce and Parmesan to the spaghetti, season with salt and pepper, and toss well with two spoons. Mix well and serve immediately.

1 tablespoon olive oil
6 oz. smoked bacon, cut into strips
1 garlic clove, crushed and chopped
10 oz. spaghetti
4 tablespoons heavy cream
3 egg yolks
3 oz. Parmesan cheese,
    freshly grated
salt and pepper

Preparation time **10 minutes**   Cooking time **10 minutes**   Total time **20 minutes**   *Serves 4*

penne with chicken livers

1 yellow pepper, cored,
halved and deseeded
10 oz. penne
2 tablespoons olive oil
4 tablespoons butter
1 red onion, sliced
8 oz. chicken livers, trimmed
sprig of rosemary, chopped
salt and pepper
3 oz. Parmesan cheese,
freshly grated, to serve

one   Place a large saucepan of water on to boil for the pasta.

two   Roast the yellow pepper in a hot oven or under the broiler for 5 minutes until the skin is blistered and black. Allow to cool, then peel away the skin. Cut the flesh into long strips.

three   Add the pasta to the boiling water and cook for 4 minutes if fresh and 8 minutes if dried, or according to package instructions.

four   Heat the oil and butter in a large skillet, add the onion and chicken livers, and cook on high heat until browned all over. Add the rosemary and season with salt and pepper. Do not overcook the chicken livers, as this dries them out and makes them hard; they are best still pink in the middle.

five   Mix the chicken liver sauce with the pasta and toss well. Serve immediately with a bowl of freshly grated Parmesan.

Preparation time **15 minutes**   Cooking time **15 minutes**
Oven temperature **400°F**
Total time **30 minutes**   *Serves 4*

pasta bake with spinach and ham

2 tablespoons olive oil
1 onion, chopped
1 garlic clove, crushed and chopped
1½ lb. fresh spinach, washed and chopped
pinch of grated nutmeg
8 sheets fresh lasagna
8 oz. ham, chopped into large chunks
4 oz. package buffalo mozzarella cheese, thinly sliced
4 oz. fontina cheese, grated
salt and pepper

one   Heat the olive oil in a saucepan, add the onion and garlic, and sauté for 3 minutes.

two   Add the spinach and mix well. Cook for 2 minutes over moderate heat, just so that the spinach starts to wilt. Add nutmeg to taste, and season with salt and pepper.

three   Lightly oil a large shallow baking dish. Place a layer of lasagna at the bottom, followed by a layer of spinach, then ham, and then a layer of mozzarella. Repeat until all the ingredients are used, finishing with lasagna and the grated fontina cheese.

four   Place the dish at the top of a preheated oven, 400°F, and bake for 15 minutes until golden brown and bubbling.

Preparation time **5 minutes**   Cooking time **20 minutes**
Total time **25 minutes**   *Serves 4*

orecchiette with spicy tomato and pancetta sauce

2 tablespoons olive oil
1 onion, chopped
2 garlic cloves, crushed and chopped
4 oz. pancetta, chopped
13 oz. can chopped tomatoes
½–1 teaspoon crushed dried chilies
½ cup red wine
10 oz. orecchiette
handful of flat-leafed parsley, chopped
handful of basil, chopped
salt and pepper
3 oz. Parmesan shavings, to garnish

one   Heat the olive oil in a saucepan, add the onion, garlic, and pancetta, and sauté for 5 minutes.

two   Add the chopped tomatoes, dried chilies, and red wine, and simmer for 15 minutes or until the sauce is rich and thick.

three   Place a large saucepan of water on to boil for the pasta.

four   Put the pasta in the boiling water, stir well, and simmer for 3 minutes if fresh and 6 minutes if dried, or according to package instructions. Drain well.

five   Stir the parsley, basil, and salt and pepper into the sauce. Add to the pasta and toss well. Garnish with some of the Parmesan shavings and serve with a separate bowl at the table.

Because this dish uses fresh lasagna and is loosely layered, it cooks through much more quickly than traditional baked lasagna.

Risotto

Traditionally, risotto is served in small portions in large wide-rimmed soup plates and topped with grated Parmesan or pecorino cheese. Sometimes risottos are simple with just the addition of fresh herbs; other times they are more substantial, cooked with seafood, meat, or vegetables. It is essential that the short-grained arborio or carnaroli rices are used for risottos.

Preparation time **10 minutes**   Cooking time **20 minutes**   Total time **30 minutes**   *Serves 4*

4 cups chicken or vegetable stock
8 tablespoons butter
1 tablespoon olive oil
1 garlic clove, crushed and chopped
1 onion, finely diced
10 oz. arborio or carnaroli rice
4 oz. green beans, trimmed and cut into
1-inch pieces
4 oz. shelled peas
4 oz. shelled and skinned fava beans
4 oz. asparagus, trimmed and cut into
1-inch pieces
4 oz. baby spinach, washed and chopped
6 tablespoons dry vermouth or white wine
2 tablespoons chopped parsley
4 oz. Parmesan cheese, freshly grated
salt and pepper

green vegetable risotto

one   Place the chicken or vegetable stock in a saucepan and simmer gently.

two   Melt 4 tablespoons of the butter with the olive oil in a heavy-based saucepan, add the garlic and onion, and sauté gently for 5 minutes; do not brown.

three   Add the rice; stir well to coat each grain with the butter and oil. Add enough stock to just cover the rice, stir again, and simmer gently, stirring as frequently as possible.

four   When most of the liquid is absorbed, add more stock; keep adding stock, stirring and simmering gently, until the stock is absorbed. When you add the last of the stock, add the vegetables and vermouth or white wine, mix well, and cook for 2 minutes.

five   Remove the pan from the heat, season with salt and pepper, and add the remaining butter, the chopped parsley, and Parmesan. Mix well and serve at once.

Preparation time **5 minutes**   Cooking time **20 minutes**   Total time **25 minutes**   *Serves 4*

risotto alla Milanese

one   Place the chicken stock in a saucepan and simmer gently.

two   Melt 4 tablespoons of the butter and the olive oil in a large heavy-based saucepan, add the onions, and sauté for 5 minutes.

three   Add the rice to the onions and stir well to coat each grain with the butter; add enough stock to just cover the rice and stir well. Simmer gently, stirring as frequently as possible.

four   When most of the liquid is absorbed, add more stock and the saffron and stir well. Continue adding the stock in stages, and stirring until it has all been absorbed.

five   Finally add the vermouth or white wine, Parmesan, and the remaining butter in small lumps and season with salt and pepper. Stir well and serve immediately.

4 cups chicken stock
6 tablespoons butter
1 tablespoon olive oil
2 onions, finely diced
14 oz. arborio or carnaroli rice
½ teaspoon saffron threads
½ cup dry vermouth or dry white wine
4 oz. Parmesan cheese, freshly grated
salt and pepper

Fresh or dried mushrooms may be used for this recipe. If you use dried mushrooms, use 4 oz. and soak them in hot water for 15 minutes to rehydrate. Use the excess liquid as stock in the recipe, as it is full of delicious flavors.

risotto with forest mushrooms and sage

4 cups vegetable stock
8 tablespoons butter
1 tablespoon olive oil
1 garlic clove, crushed and chopped
1 onion, finely diced
8 oz. forest (wild) mushrooms, e.g.
morel, porcini, chanterelle, or
common open mushroom,
halved or quartered
10 oz. arborio or carnaroli rice
6 tablespoons dry white wine
1 tablespoon chopped sage
salt and pepper
4 oz. Parmesan cheese,
freshly grated, to serve
truffle oil, to drizzle (optional)

one   Pour the stock into a saucepan and simmer gently.

two   Heat half the butter with the oil in a heavy-based saucepan, add the garlic and onion, and sauté gently for 3 minutes; do not brown.

three   Add the mushrooms to the onions and continue to cook gently for 2 minutes.

four   Add the rice and mix well so that all the grains are coated in the oil and butter.

five   Add just enough stock to cover the rice, stir well, and simmer gently, stirring as frequently as possible throughout cooking. As the liquid evaporates, continue to add ladles of stock to just cover the rice, and stir well.

six   Finally add the white wine, the remaining butter, the sage, and salt and pepper to the rice and stir well. Serve with the Parmesan in a separate bowl and drizzle with truffle oil, if desired.

Preparation time **5 minutes**   Cooking time **20 minutes**
Total time **25 minutes**   *Serves 4*

red wine risotto

2½ cups chicken stock
1½ cups Valpolicella or other
red wine
1 tablespoon olive oil
8 tablespoons butter
2 garlic cloves, crushed and
chopped
2 red onions, chopped
10 oz. arborio or carnaroli rice
8 oz. field mushrooms, sliced
6 oz. Parmesan cheese,
freshly grated
salt and pepper

one   Heat the stock and red wine in a large saucepan to a gentle simmer.

two   Heat the olive oil and 4 tablespoons of the butter in a heavy-based saucepan. Add the garlic and onions and sauté gently for 5 minutes; do not brown.

three   Add the rice and mix well to coat the grains with the butter and oil. Add enough of the hot stock to cover the rice, stir well, and simmer gently. Continue to stir as frequently as possible throughout cooking. As the liquid is absorbed, add more stock by the ladle to just cover the rice, stirring well.

four   When half of the stock has been incorporated, add the mushrooms and season with salt and pepper. The rice should be stained with the color of the wine, giving it a rich dark red color.

five   When all the stock has been added, and the rice is just cooked with a good creamy sauce, add most of the Parmesan and the remaining butter and mix well. Garnish with a little grated Parmesan and serve with the rest of the bottle of red wine.

Preparation time **5 minutes**   Cooking time **25 minutes**
Oven Temperature: **425°F**   Total time **30 minutes**   *Serves 4*

butternut squash risotto

1 butternut squash, weighing 2 lbs.
3 tablespoons olive oil
4 cups chicken or vegetable stock
8 tablespoons butter
1 garlic clove, crushed and chopped
1 onion, finely diced
10 oz. arborio or carnaroli rice
5 oz. Parmesan cheese, freshly grated
salt and pepper
pumpkin seed oil, to serve

one   Trim the ends from the squash, cut in half around the middle, then pare away the skin from the larger half without losing too much of the flesh. Cut in half lengthwise, remove the seeds, and cut into 2-inch cubes. Repeat with the other half. Place on a large baking sheet, drizzle with 2 tablespoons of the olive oil, and season with salt and pepper. Mix well and cook in the top of a preheated oven at 425°F for 15 minutes. The squash should be soft and slightly browned.

two   Meanwhile, heat the stock to a gentle simmer in a saucepan.

three   Melt the remaining olive oil and 4 tablespoons of the butter in a heavy-based saucepan, add the garlic and onion, and sauté gently for 5 minutes; do not brown.

four   Add the rice, stir well to coat the grains with oil and butter, then add enough stock to cover the rice. Stir well and simmer gently. Continue to stir as frequently as possible throughout cooking. As the liquid is absorbed, continue to add ladles of stock to just cover the rice, and stir well.

five   Remove the squash from the oven, add to the risotto with the Parmesan and the remaining butter, season with salt and pepper, and stir gently.

six   Serve the risotto on individual warmed plates with a little pumpkin seed oil drizzled on top of each portion.

Preparation time **5 minutes**   Cooking time **20 minutes**   Total time **25 minutes**   *Serves 4*

green herb risotto

4 cups chicken or vegetable stock
8 tablespoons butter
2 tablespoons olive oil
1 onion, finely chopped
1 garlic clove, crushed and chopped
10 oz. arborio or carnaroli rice
handful of parsley, chopped
handful of basil, chopped
handful of oregano, chopped
handful of thyme, chopped
4 oz. Toma cheese, grated
salt and pepper
herb sprigs, to garnish

one   Heat the stock in a saucepan to a gentle simmer.

two   Melt 4 tablespoons of the butter with the olive oil in a saucepan, add the onion and garlic, and sauté for 3 minutes.

three   Add the rice, stir well to coat the grains with the butter and oil, then add a ladle of stock, enough to cover the rice, and stir well. Simmer gently and continue to stir as frequently as possible, adding more stock as it is absorbed. Continue adding the stock and stirring until it has all been absorbed and the rice is cooked with a rich creamy sauce.

four   Add the herbs, the remaining butter, and the cheese. Season with salt and pepper and stir well. Serve immediately, garnished with the herb sprigs.

Toma cheese is made in the Italian Alps. If you cannot find it, use fontina or Parmesan instead.

Preparation time **5 minutes**   Cooking time **20 minutes**   Total time **25 minutes**   *Serves 4*

spinach and lemon risotto

4 cups chicken or vegetable stock
8 tablespoons butter
1 tablespoon olive oil
2 shallots, finely chopped
10 oz. arborio or carnaroli rice
1 lb. spinach, chopped
grated rind and juice of 1 lemon
4 oz. Parmesan cheese, freshly grated
salt and pepper
grated lemon rind, to garnish (optional)

one   Heat the stock in a saucepan to a gentle simmer.

two   Melt 4 tablespoons of the butter and the olive oil in a saucepan, add the shallots, and sauté for 3 minutes.

three   Add the rice and stir well to coat the grains thoroughly with butter and oil. Add a ladleful of stock, enough to cover the rice, and stir well. Simmer gently and continue to stir as frequently as possible, adding more stock as it is absorbed.

four   Before you add the last of the stock, stir in the chopped spinach, lemon rind and juice, and season with salt and pepper. Increase the heat, stir well, then add the remaining stock and butter. Allow to cook for a few minutes, then add half of the Parmesan and mix in well. Serve garnished with the remaining Parmesan and grated lemon rind, if desired.

Preparation time **10 minutes**   Cooking time **20 minutes**
Total time **30 minutes**   *Serves 4*

seafood risotto

4 cups fish, chicken, or vegetable stock
good pinch of saffron threads
8 tablespoons butter
2 tablespoons olive oil
3 shallots, chopped
1 garlic clove, crushed and chopped
10 oz. arborio or carnaroli rice
4 oz. small scallops, removed from their shells
4 oz. prepared squid, cut into rings
4 oz. peeled shrimp
2 tablespoons coarsely chopped flat-leafed parsley
¼ cup plus 2 tablespoons white wine or dry vermouth
4 oz. Parmesan cheese, freshly grated
salt and pepper

one   Heat the stock and saffron in a saucepan to a gentle simmer.

two   Melt 4 tablespoons of the butter and 1 tablespoon of the olive oil in another saucepan, add the shallots and garlic, and sauté for 5 minutes; do not let them brown.

three   Add the rice and stir well to coat the grains thoroughly with the butter and oil. Pour in enough hot stock to cover the rice, stir well, and simmer gently. Continue stirring as frequently as possible throughout the cooking. As the liquid is absorbed, add more stock by the ladle to just cover the rice, and stir well.

four   When half of the stock has been incorporated, add the scallops, squid, and shrimp, turn the heat up a little, and continue to add the stock by the ladle; stir carefully so as not to break up the seafood.

five   When all the stock has been absorbed, add the parsley, the remaining butter, white wine or vermouth, half of the Parmesan, and season with salt and pepper. Stir well. Serve garnished with the remaining Parmesan.

The secret of a good risotto is to cook it very slowly over low heat until all the liquid has been absorbed and the rice is plump and tender.

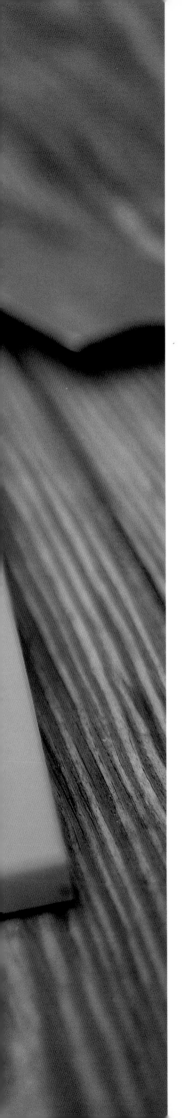

Pizza
and Polenta

Naples is reputed to be the original home of the pizza, but pizzas are now found all over Italy. Polenta is a yellow corn flour from northern Italy that can be baked, broiled, used as an accompaniment, or is delicious with the addition of cheese.

Preparation time **10 minutes**   Cooking time **see recipes**   *Makes 4*

quick pizza base

2 cups self-rising flour
1 teaspoon salt
½ cup plus 2 tablespoons warm water

It is very important to cook the pizza bases in a very hot oven, so be sure to turn the oven on well in advance to preheat it before you bake the pizzas.

one   Place the flour and salt in a large bowl and mix well. Slowly add the water and mix to form a soft dough. When it has bound together, mix the dough with your hands into a ball. Turn the dough out on a lightly floured surface and knead until smooth and soft.

two   Divide the dough in to 4, and with your hands and a rolling pin, flatten it as thinly as possible. The pizza rounds do not have to be exact circles as that is one of the charms of making your own pizzas! Make the pizzas just a bit smaller than your serving plates and as thin as you can.

Preparation time **8–10 minutes, plus preparing the pizza base**   Cooking time **10 minutes**
Oven temperature **450°F**   Total time **30 minutes**   *Serves 4*

classic tomato pizza

1 recipe Quick Pizza Base (see above)
3 tablespoons olive oil
2 red onions, sliced finely
2 garlic cloves, crushed and chopped
2 x 13 oz. cans chopped tomatoes
1 teaspoon red wine vinegar
sugar, to taste
8 anchovy fillets, cut in to thin lengths
2 tablespoons pitted black olives
1 tablespoon capers
8 oz. mozzarella cheese, sliced
salt and pepper

one   Roll out the dough into four circles or a large square.

two   Heat the oil in a large saucepan, add the onion and garlic, and sauté for 3 minutes. Add the tomatoes, vinegar, and sugar and season with salt and pepper. Increase the heat and simmer the mixture until it has reduced by half to make a thick and rich tomato sauce.

three   Place the pizza bases on warmed baking sheets, spoon the sauce over, and spread to the edge with the back of the spoon.

four   Arrange the anchovies on the pizzas, sprinkle with the olives and capers, and finally add the mozzarella. Put the pizzas into a preheated oven, 450°F, and cook for 10 minutes until golden and sizzling.

If you do not have enough baking sheets or space in your oven, make a large square pizza and serve it cut into squares.

Preparation time **8–10 minutes**, plus preparing the pizza base
Cooking time **10–15 minutes**   Oven temperature **450°F**
Total time **30 minutes**   *Serves 4*

fresh wild mushroom pizza

1 recipe Quick Pizza Base (see page 50)
olive oil, for brushing
2 onions, finely sliced
2 garlic cloves, crushed and chopped
8 oz. wild mushrooms, sliced
drizzle of truffle oil
salt and pepper
handful of flat-leafed parsley, chopped, to garnish

one   Put the pizza bases onto warmed baking sheets and brush them lightly with olive oil.

two   Mix together the onions, garlic, and mushrooms, and season with salt and pepper. Spread the mixture over the pizzas and drizzle with a scant amount of truffle oil. Put the pizzas into a preheated oven, 450°F, and bake for 10–15 minutes.

three   Sprinkle the pizzas with parsley and serve immediately.

Preparation time **8–10 minutes**, plus preparing the pizza base
Cooking time **10–15 minutes**
Oven temperature **450°F**
Total time **30 minutes**   *Serves 4*

artichoke and goat cheese pizza

1 recipe Quick Pizza Base
(see page 50)
2 onions, sliced finely
2 lb. artichokes in oil
2 tablespoons pitted black olives
6 oz. mild goat cheese, cut into
thin slices or crumbled
handful of oregano, chopped
salt and pepper

one   Put the pizza bases onto warmed baking sheets.

two   Mix together the onions and artichokes and season well with salt and pepper.

three   Divide the mixture between the bases and spread over evenly. Sprinkle with the olives and top with the goat cheese, oregano, and salt and pepper. Put the pizzas in a preheated oven, 450°F, and bake for 10–15 minutes.

The addition of 2 oz. of wild mushrooms, such as chanterelles, to this pizza makes it really special.

Preparation time **20 minutes, plus preparing the pizza base**   Cooking time **10 minutes**
Oven temperature **450°F**   Total time **30 minutes**   *Serves 4*

fresh vegetable pizza

1 recipe Quick Pizza Base (see page 50)
5 tablespoons olive oil
2 garlic cloves, crushed and chopped
1 red onion, finely sliced
2 zucchini, thinly sliced lengthwise
1 red pepper, cored, deseeded, and cut into thin strips
1 yellow pepper, cored, deseeded, and cut into thin strips
4 plum tomatoes, skinned, cored, and cut into small wedges
1 lb. asparagus, trimmed
4 thyme sprigs, separated into leaves
handful of basil leaves, roughly torn
salt and pepper
3 oz. fresh Parmesan shavings (optional), to serve

one   Put the pizza bases onto warmed baking sheets, brush with a little olive oil, then arrange the vegetables on the bases, sprinkling them with the thyme leaves and roughly torn basil.

two   Season the pizzas generously with salt and pepper, drizzle with olive oil, and bake at the top of a preheated oven, 450°F, for 10 minutes. The vegetables should be slightly charred around the edges as this adds to the flavor. Serve with fresh Parmesan shavings, if desired.

Preparation time **8 minutes, plus preparing the pizza base**   Cooking time **10 minutes**
Oven temperature **450°F**   Total time **18 minutes**   *Serves 4*

anchovy and red pepper pizza

one   Heat the olive oil in a saucepan, add the onions and red peppers, and cook for about 5 minutes until soft. Add the garlic and mix well.

two   Put the pizza bases onto warmed baking sheets and spoon and spread the cooked peppers over them. Arrange the anchovies on top and sprinkle with salt and pepper, chopped marjoram, and olives, and add the slices of mozzarella.

three   Put the pizzas into a preheated oven, 450°F, and bake for 10 minutes.

4 tablespoons olive oil
2 red onions, sliced
4 red peppers, cored, deseeded, and cut into strips
2 garlic cloves, crushed and chopped
1 recipe Quick Pizza Base (see page 50)
2 oz. can anchovies
handful of marjoram, chopped
1 tablespoon black olives, pitted and chopped
8 oz. buffalo mozzarella, sliced
salt and pepper

Preparation time **5 minutes**   Cooking time **about 15 minutes**
Total time **20 minutes**   *Serves 4*

creamed polenta
with dolcelatte and mascarpone

2½ cups water
1¼ cup quick-cooking
polenta flour
4 tablespoons butter
2 tablespoons olive oil
6 oz. dolcelatte and
mascarpone torta
handful of oregano,
chopped
salt and pepper

one   Heat the water to a gentle simmer, pour in the polenta, and beat well for 1–2 minutes until it becomes a smooth paste.

two   Turn the heat down and continue to cook the polenta until it thickens, stirring constantly so that it does not stick to the bottom of the pan or form a skin on the top; it needs to cook in this way for 6–8 minutes.

three   When it is thick and cooked, add the salt and pepper, the butter, and olive oil, and mix well. The dolcelatte and mascarpone torta is very creamy and wet; break it up into small pieces and add to the polenta with the oregano. Mix well.

four   The polenta should now be the consistency of soft mashed potatoes. Serve on its own or with broiled chicken breasts.

Preparation time **15 minutes, plus preparing the pizza base**
Cooking time **13–15 minutes**   Oven temperature **450°F**
Total time **30 minutes**   *Serves 4*

1 recipe Quick Pizza Base (see page 50)
olive oil, for brushing and drizzling
2 onions, finely sliced
2 garlic cloves, peeled and sliced
4 tomatoes, skinned and sliced
8 oz. spinach, cooked and chopped
8 slices Parma ham, cut into strips
1 tablespoon black olives, pitted and
chopped
4 eggs
salt and pepper

spinach,
Parma ham,
and egg
pizza

one   Put the pizza bases onto warmed baking sheets. Brush them lightly with olive oil and season with salt and pepper.

two   Mix together the onions, garlic, tomatoes, spinach, Parma ham, and olives and spread over the bases, making a nest in the middle of each one for the egg.

three   Drizzle the pizzas with olive oil and season with salt and pepper. Place in a preheated oven, 450°F, and cook for 10 minutes, then remove from the oven and crack the eggs into the nests. Return the pizzas to the oven for 3–5 minutes, then serve immediately. If you like your egg hard, put it on the vegetable topping when it first goes in the oven.

Polenta has to be stirred continuously during cooking or it will become lumpy. Use instant or quick-cooking polenta for these recipes.

Preparation time **10 minutes**
Cooking time **20 minutes**
Oven temperature **400°F**
Total time **30 minutes**   *Serves 4*

baked polenta
with fontina

2½ cups water
1¼ cup quick-cooking polenta flour
8 tablespoons butter
handful of marjoram, chopped
7 oz. fontina cheese, grated
salt and pepper
Sauce:
3 tablespoons olive oil
2 garlic cloves, crushed and chopped
1 onion, chopped
13 oz. can chopped tomatoes
1 thyme sprig
1 teaspoon vinegar
1 teaspoon sugar

one   Heat the water to a gentle simmer, pour in the polenta flour, and beat well for 1–2 minutes until it is a smooth paste.

two   Turn the heat down and continue to cook the polenta until it thickens, stirring constantly so that it does not stick to the bottom of the pan or form a skin on the top; it needs to cook in this way for 6–8 minutes.

three   When the polenta is thick and cooked, add the butter, chopped marjoram, and season with salt and pepper. Mix well. Place the polenta on a chopping board, roll out to ¾-inch thick, and allow to set for 5 minutes. Alternatively, shape into a loaf and slice into ¾-inch thick slices.

four   To make the sauce, heat the olive oil in a saucepan, add the garlic and onion, and sauté for 3 minutes.

five   Add the tomatoes, thyme, vinegar, and sugar. Season with salt and pepper and simmer for 10 minutes over moderate to high heat until the tomatoes reduce to make a thick sauce.

six   Butter a shallow ovenproof dish, cut the polenta into squares, and line the bottom of the dish with half of the squares. Sprinkle half of the grated fontina over. Spoon half of the sauce over and top with the remaining polenta. Add the remaining sauce and the remaining grated fontina and bake in a preheated oven, 400°F, for 10–15 minutes until the cheese is golden and the sauce bubbling.

Preparation time **5 minutes**   Cooking time **25 minutes**   Total time **30 minutes**   *Serves 4*

broiled polenta with asparagus
and Parmesan

2½ cups water
1¼ cup quick-cooking polenta flour
4 tablespoons butter
1 lb. asparagus, trimmed
3 tablespoons olive oil
1 tablespoon balsamic vinegar
salt and pepper
4 oz. Parmesan shavings, to garnish

Parmesan shavings are best made with a mandolin, but you can also use a vegetable peeler. Shave the Parmesan straight onto the prepared dish, as the shavings are very fragile and do not handle well.

one   Heat the water to a gentle simmer, pour in the polenta flour, and beat well for 1–2 minutes until it is a smooth paste.

two   Turn the heat down and continue to cook the polenta until it thickens, stirring constantly so that it does not stick to the bottom of the pan or form a skin on the top; it needs to cook in this way for 6–8 minutes. When it is thick and cooked, add the salt and pepper and the butter; mix well.

three   Turn the polenta onto a chopping board, roll out to ¾-inch thick, and allow to set for 5 minutes.

four   A griddle pan or a broiler can be used to finish this dish. Heat the griddle pan until it is hot or turn the broiler on to high to heat up.

five   Cut the polenta into wedges, and cook on each side for 5 minutes. If you are using a griddle it will be easier to get a good color, but this does not affect the taste.

six   Broil or griddle-cook the asparagus for 4–5 minutes on high heat, turning it as it colors.

seven   To serve, arrange the polenta on a warmed serving dish and place the asparagus on top. Drizzle with the olive oil and balsamic vinegar and garnish with the Parmesan shavings.

Preparation time **10 minutes**   Cooking time **20 minutes**
Total time **30 minutes**   *Serves 4*

rich polenta salad

2½ cups water
1¼ cup quick-cooking polenta flour
2 tablespoons butter
8 oz. goat cheese, rind removed
1 small radicchio lettuce, separated into leaves
4 oz. arugula
3 tablespoons extra virgin olive oil
1 tablespoon balsamic vinegar
salt and pepper

one   Heat the water to a gentle simmer, pour in the polenta flour, and beat well for 1–2 minutes until it is a smooth paste. Turn the heat down and continue to cook the polenta until it thickens, stirring constantly so that it does not stick to the bottom of the pan or form a skin on the top; it needs to cook in this way for 6–8 minutes.

two   When the polenta is thick and cooked, add the butter and season with salt and pepper; mix well. Place it on a chopping board and spread to ¾-inch thick and allow to set for 5 minutes.

three   Slice thinly or crumble the goat cheese and arrange it on the polenta, then cut the polenta into bars or wedges. Place the polenta under a preheated broiler and cook until the cheese has melted and starts to bubble.

four   Put the radicchio leaves and the arugula into a bowl. Add the oil and vinegar and season with salt and pepper, then toss the leaves until coated. Arrange the salad leaves on individual plates and place the polenta bars on top.

Preparation time **5 minutes**   Cooking time **25 minutes**   Total time **30 minutes**   *Serves 4*

grilled polenta with mushrooms and Parma ham

one   Heat the water to a gentle simmer, pour in the polenta flour, and beat well for 1–2 minutes until it is a smooth paste.

two   Turn the heat down and continue to cook the polenta until it thickens. Keep stirring constantly so that it does not stick to the bottom of the pan or form a skin on the top; it needs to cook in this way for 6–8 minutes.

three   When the polenta is thick and cooked, add 4 tablespoons of the butter and season with salt and pepper; mix well. Turn the polenta onto a chopping board, roll out to ¾-inch thick and allow to set for 5 minutes.

four   Melt the remaining butter in a saucepan with the olive oil. Add the garlic, mushrooms, and thyme and sauté for 10 minutes with the wine, to keep them moist. Season with salt and pepper.

five   Cut the polenta into wedges, place on a preheated griddle or under a hot broiler, and cook for 5 minutes on each side.

six   Serve the polenta with the Parma ham draped over and the mushrooms spooned over to one side. This dish can be served hot or at room temperature.

2½ cups water
1¼ cup quick-cooking polenta flour
8 tablespoons butter
1 tablespoons olive oil
1 garlic clove, crushed and chopped
12 oz. mushrooms, sliced
½ teaspoon chopped thyme
½ cup dry white wine
8 thin slices Parma ham
salt and pepper

The best goat cheese to use for this recipe is the rindless, soft, spreadable variety. The hard-crusted goat cheese can be used, but it is not as easy to spread.

Salads

The majority of salads in this chapter can be main meals in their own right, but many make great accompaniments or appetizers, too.

Preparation time **20 minutes**   Cooking time **5 minutes**
Total time **25 minutes**   *Serves 4*

Caesar salad

one   Place the garlic, anchovy fillets, lemon juice, mustard, and egg yolk in a small mixing bowl and season with pepper. With a hand-held blender or small whisk, mix well until combined. Slowly drizzle in the olive oil, mixing all the time to form a thick creamy sauce. If the sauce is too thick, add a little water.

two   Heat the vegetable oil in a skillet. Test with a small piece of bread to see if it is hot enough; if the bread sizzles, add the croutons, turning them when they are golden. When they are cooked, transfer them to a plate lined with paper towels to absorb the excess oil.

three   Put the lettuce into a large bowl, pour the dressing over, add 2 tablespoons of the Parmesan, and mix well.

four   Serve the salad in a large bowl or on individual plates, sprinkled with the croutons and the remaining Parmesan.

1 garlic clove, peeled and crushed
4 anchovy fillets, chopped
juice of 1 lemon
2 teaspoons dry English mustard
1 egg yolk
¾ cup plus 2 tablespoons extra virgin
    olive oil
vegetable oil for frying
3 slices country bread, cubed
1 romaine lettuce, washed and torn
    into pieces
3 tablespoons freshly grated
    Parmesan cheese
pepper

Preparation time **15 minutes**   Total time **15 minutes**   *Serves 4*

panzanella

When making this delicious but very simple salad dish, try to cut all the ingredients into a similar size. This salad makes a great appetizer or a side dish to serve with a summer fish dinner.

one   Cut or tear the bread into small pieces and place them in a large bowl.

two   Remove the green core from the tomatoes. Cut them up and add to the bread.

three   Cut the cucumber in quarters lengthwise, and then into cubes. Add to the salad. Chop the onion and add to the bowl with the parsley and olives.

four   Mix together the olive oil, vinegar, lemon juice, and season with salt and pepper. Pour the dressing over the salad and mix well. Cover and let stand at room temperature for at least 1 hour before serving, to allow all the flavors to steep and mingle.

4 slices ciabatta bread
4 ripe tomatoes
½ cucumber, peeled
1 red onion
handful of chopped flat-leafed parsley
1 tablespoon chopped black olives
4 tablespoons extra virgin olive oil
1–2 tablespoons wine vinegar
juice of ½ lemon
salt and pepper

All the ingredients for this dish can be prepared in advance, but never mix the salad until it is needed, as the lettuce will become soggy.

Preparation time **10 minutes**   Cooking time **2 minutes**   Total time **12 minutes**   *Serves 4*

tomato and green bean salad

8 oz. mixed red and yellow baby
tomatoes, plum if possible
8 oz. thin green beans, ends trimmed
handful of mint, chopped
1 garlic clove, crushed and chopped
4 tablespoons extra virgin olive oil
1 tablespoons balsamic vinegar
salt and pepper

one   Cut the baby tomatoes in half and place in a large bowl.

two   Cook the green beans in boiling water for 2 minutes, then drain well and place in the large bowl with the tomatoes.

three   Add the chopped mint, garlic, olive oil, and balsamic vinegar. Season with salt and pepper and mix well. Serve warm or cold.

white bean and sun-dried tomato salad

Preparation time **10 minutes**
Cooking time **5 minutes**
Total time **15 minutes**   *Serves 4*

one   Heat the oil in a skillet, add the onion and garlic, and sauté over high heat, stirring, to gain a little color. When they are golden, remove from the pan.

two   Put the beans into a mixing bowl and stir in the onion and garlic. Add the sun-dried tomatoes, olives, capers, thyme, extra virgin olive oil, lemon juice, and salt and pepper to taste and mix well. Check the seasoning and serve.

2 tablespoons olive oil
1 onion, sliced
1 garlic clove, crushed and chopped
14 oz. can white beans, drained
4 oz. sun-dried tomatoes in oil,
drained and coarsely chopped
1 tablespoon chopped black olives
2 teaspoons chopped capers
2 teaspoons chopped thyme
1 tablespoon extra virgin olive oil
juice of ½ lemon
salt and pepper

Preparation time **10 minutes**   Cooking time **2 minutes**   Total time **12 minutes**   *Serves 4*

new season fava bean and pecorino salad

12 oz. shelled fresh
fava beans
6 oz. pecorino cheese
2 tablespoons extra
virgin olive oil
juice of ½ lemon
1 tablespoon chopped
flat-leafed parsley
salt and pepper

one   Blanch the beans in boiling water for 2 minutes. Drain and refresh. If you have the time, after blanching the beans, remove the outer skins to reveal the bright green, velvety bean inside.

two   Grate the cheese on the coarse grid of the grater and put it in a mixing bowl. Add the beans, olive oil, lemon juice, and parsley, season with salt and pepper, and mix well. Serve as part of an antipasto.

This salad makes a tasty meal on its own,
as well as being an ideal accompaniment
to broiled meat or fish.

Preparation time **10 minutes**   Cooking time **10 minutes**
Oven temperature **375°F**
Total time **20 minutes**   *Serves 4*

eggplant, tomato, and mozzarella mountains

1 eggplant, cut into 8 slices
4 beefsteak tomatoes, skinned, then cut into 8 slices
8 oz. package buffalo mozzarella, cut into 8 slices
2 tablespoons olive oil
Pesto (see page 16)
salt and pepper
mint sprigs, to garnish

one   Arrange the eggplant slices on a preheated griddle or under a hot broiler and cook until browned on both sides.

two   Lightly oil a baking sheet.

three   To prepare the stacks, place four of the eggplant slices on the baking sheet. Put a tomato slice and a mozzarella slice on each one, then make a second layer of eggplant, tomato, and mozzarella, sprinkling each layer with salt and pepper as you go. Skewer with a toothpick through the center to hold the stacks together.

four   Place the stacks in a preheated oven, 375°F, and cook for 10 minutes.

five   To serve, transfer the stacks onto individual serving plates and carefully remove the toothpicks. Drizzle with a little olive oil and top with a generous spoonful of pesto. Garnish with mint sprigs and serve warm or at room temperature.

Preparation time **10 minutes**
Cooking time **20 minutes**
Total time **30 minutes**
Serves 4

caponata

This salad actually improves if allowed to stand.

6 tablespoons olive oil
2 eggplants, cubed
1 red onion, chopped
3 celery stalks, chopped
5 tomatoes, skinned and coarsely chopped
3 tablespoons red wine vinegar
1 tablespoon sugar
1 tablespoon capers
2 oz. black olives, pitted
handful of flat-leafed parsley, chopped
salt and pepper

one   Heat the oil in a saucepan, add the eggplants, and fry until golden and soft. Remove from the pan and drain on paper towels.

two   Add the onion and celery to the pan and sauté for 6 minutes until soft but not brown.

three   Add the tomatoes and cook for 3 minutes, then add the vinegar, sugar, capers, olives, parsley, and season with salt and pepper. Simmer for 5 minutes. Remove the pan from the heat, add the eggplants, and mix well. Allow to cool, then serve.

Serve these "mountains" with crusty Italian
bread to mop up the delicious pesto juices.

Serve this eggplant
salad as an appetizer or
as an accompaniment.

Preparation time **10 minutes, plus cooling**   Cooking time **15 minutes**
Total time **25 minutes**   *Serves 4*

eggplant salad

4 tablespoons olive oil
1 onion, chopped
2 garlic cloves, crushed and chopped
2 eggplants, cubed
4 tomatoes, peeled and coarsely chopped
4 anchovy fillets, chopped
2 tablespoons pitted black olives
3 oz. pine nuts, toasted
2 tablespoons chopped capers
handful of flat-leafed parsley, chopped
salt and pepper
Italian salad dressing:
1 tablespoon white wine vinegar
3 tablespoons olive oil
juice of ½ lemon
1 teaspoon Dijon mustard

one   Heat the olive oil in a saucepan, add the onion, garlic, and eggplants, and sauté for 15 minutes.

two   Meanwhile, make the Italian salad dressing. Place all the ingredients in a jar with a lid, season with salt and pepper, and shake well. Set aside.

three   Add the tomatoes, anchovies, olives, pine nuts, capers, and parsley to the eggplant mixture, and season with salt and pepper. Pour in the salad dressing, mix well, then allow the salad to cool.

Preparation time **5 minutes, plus cooling**   Cooking time **25 minutes**
Oven temperature **400°F**   Total time **30 minutes**   *Serves 4*

Piedmont peppers

4 red peppers
4–8 anchovy fillets
4 tomatoes, skinned and quartered
4 tablespoons olive oil
salt and pepper
To garnish:
handful of green or red basil,
roughly torn
4 oz. Parmesan cheese

one   Cut the peppers in half lengthwise. Cut through the stalk first and then the flesh. I always leave the stalk on, as it looks attractive. Remove the seeds and the white ribs.

two   Lightly oil a baking sheet and place the peppers on it, skin side down.

three   Cut the anchovies into halves or quarters lengthwise, depending on how much you like anchovies.

four   Put 2 tomato quarters into each red pepper, make an anchovy cross on top, and drizzle with olive oil. Sprinkle with salt and pepper and place in a preheated oven, 400°F, and cook for 25 minutes.

five   Allow the peppers to cool, then serve garnished with torn basil and Parmesan shavings. Shave the Parmesan straight onto the peppers, using a mandoline or a vegetable peeler, as it does not handle well.

Preparation time **15 minutes**
Total time **15 minutes**
Serves 4

arugula, tuna, and navy bean salad

4 tomatoes, skinned, cored, and coarsely chopped
4 oz. arugula
14 oz. can navy beans, drained
7 oz. can tuna in olive oil
1 red onion, chopped
4 oz. artichoke hearts in olive oil
2 young celery stalks with leaves, chopped
1 tablespoon pitted black olives
juice of 1 lemon
1 tablespoon red wine vinegar
¼ teaspoon crushed dried chili
handful of flat-leafed parsley, coarsely chopped
salt and pepper

one   Put the tomatoes into a large salad bowl with the arugula.

two   Stir in the navy beans and the tuna and olive oil, roughly breaking up the tuna into large flakes. Stir in the chopped red onion.

three   Add the artichoke hearts and their olive oil, celery, olives, lemon juice, red wine vinegar, crushed dried chili, parsley, and season with salt and pepper.

four   Mix all the ingredients together well and allow to stand for 30 minutes for the flavors to mingle. Serve at room temperature with warm crusty bread.

Preparation time **10 minutes**   Cooking time **15 minutes**   Total time **25 minutes**   *Serves 4*

chicken and Parmesan salad

one   Place the chicken breasts on a hot griddle pan or under a preheated hot broiler and cook on each side for 5 minutes.

two   Put the garlic, olive oil, anchovies, lemon juice, mustard, and egg yolk into a blender, season with pepper, and mix until blended.

three   Put the romaine lettuce into a large bowl, pour in the dressing, and toss.

four   Arrange the lettuce on serving plates and sprinkle with torn basil leaves and the croutons.

five   Slice the chicken into long lengths and place on top of the lettuce. Shave the Parmesan onto the chicken with a mandoline or vegetable peeler and serve.

2 skinless, boneless chicken breasts
1 garlic clove, crushed and chopped
½ cup olive oil
3 anchovy fillets, coarsely chopped
juice of ½ lemon
1 teaspoon English mustard powder
1 egg yolk
1 romaine lettuce, torn into pieces
handful of basil, roughly torn
3 slices ciabatta or white country
    bread, cubed and fried in oil
3 oz. Parmesan cheese
pepper

Preparation time **5 minutes, plus 5 minutes standing**
Total time **10 minutes**   *Serves 4*

figs with Parma ham

4 figs
juice of ½ lemon
4 tablespoons extra virgin olive oil
handful of basil, roughly torn.
12 slices Parma ham, cut into paper-thin
    slices
salt and pepper

one   Cut the figs into quarters and remove the stems. Place them in a dish with the lemon juice, olive oil, roughly torn basil leaves, and season with salt and pepper. Mix well and allow to stand for 5 minutes.

two   Arrange the Parma ham on a serving plate, then spoon the figs over the ham. Sprinkle with salt and pepper and serve at room temperature.

This recipe is very simple and relies heavily on the quality of ingredients used, so it is best made when figs are in season and then only if they look ripe and delicious. It is also important to buy your Parma ham from a delicatessen where the ham is carved to order. If you like, the figs can be replaced with a fragrant, ripe melon, peeled, deseeded, and cut into wedges.

Vegetables

In Italy, vegetables appear at many different stages of the meal: as antipasti, in soups, as accompaniments, and as main courses. Italy is blessed with an abundance of different vegetables including baby artichokes, asparagus, spinach, and fennel.

Preparation time **10 minutes**   Cooking time **10 minutes**   Total time **20 minutes**   *Serves 4*

quick spinach

1 tablespoon olive oil
1 red onion, sliced
1 garlic clove, crushed and chopped
3 oz. pine nuts
4 tomatoes, peeled, cored, and coarsely chopped
2 lb. spinach, washed and trimmed
4 tablespoons butter
pinch of nutmeg
salt and pepper

one   Heat the oil in a large saucepan, add the onion and garlic, and sauté for 5 minutes.

two   Put the pine nuts into a heavy-bottomed skillet and dry-fry until browned, stirring all the time as they cook very quickly. Set aside.

three   Add the tomatoes, spinach, butter, nutmeg, and season with salt and pepper; turn up the heat to high and mix well. Cook for 3 minutes until the spinach has just started to wilt. Remove the pan from the heat, stir in the pine nuts, and serve immediately.

If you have to wash the spinach, make sure that it is dry before you start to cook. Place it in a salad spinner or dishtowel, and spin it around to disperse any excess water.

Preparation time **5 minutes**
Cooking time **10 minutes**
Total time **15 minutes**
Serves 4

fried zucchini with chilies

1½ lb. zucchini, thickly sliced
¾ cup all-purpose flour
oil, for frying
4 tablespoons butter
½ teaspoon crushed dried chilies
2 garlic cloves, crushed and chopped
juice and rind of 1 lemon
1 tablespoon green olives, pitted and chopped
salt and pepper

one   Dust the zucchini slices all over with flour.

two   Heat the oil in a skillet and fry the zucchini, in batches, for 2 minutes on each side, until golden. Remove from the pan and keep warm.

three   When all the zucchini are cooked, pour off the oil from the pan. Add the butter, chilies, garlic, lemon juice and rind, and the green olives and heat until the butter is foaming. Pour over the zucchini, season with salt and pepper, and toss. Serve immediately.

Preparation time **10 minutes**   Cooking time **12 minutes**   Total time **22 minutes**   *Serves 4*

zucchini fritters

1 lb. zucchini, trimmed and grated
1 garlic clove, crushed and chopped
2 oz. Parmesan cheese, freshly grated
¾ cup all-purpose flour
1 egg, beaten
olive oil, for frying
salt and pepper
1 lemon, cut into 4 wedges, to serve

one   Mix together the grated zucchini, garlic, Parmesan, flour, and beaten egg in a large bowl and season with salt and pepper.

two   Heat the olive oil in a skillet. Place spoonfuls of the zucchini mixture in the hot oil and fry for about 4—5 minutes on each side or until golden and crisp.

three   As the fritters are done, lift them out of the pan with a slotted spoon and pile in a warmed serving dish and keep warm. Keep cooking until all the zucchini mixture is used up.

four   Serve the fritters sprinkled with salt and accompanied by lemon wedges.

The vegetables in this dish take on a wonderful brown color from the balsamic vinegar.

Preparation time **5 minutes**   Cooking time **20 minutes**   Total time **25 minutes**   *Serves 4*

balsamic braised leeks and peppers

2 tablespoons olive oil
2 leeks, cut into ½-inch pieces
1 orange pepper, cored, deseeded,
and cut into ½-inch chunks
1 red pepper, cored, deseeded, and
cut into ½-inch chunks
3 tablespoons balsamic vinegar
handful of flat-leafed parsley,
chopped
salt and pepper

one   Heat the olive oil in a saucepan, add the leeks and orange and red peppers, stir well, cover the pan, and cook very gently for 10 minutes.

two   Add the balsamic vinegar and cook for a further 10 minutes without a lid. The vegetables should be brown from the vinegar and all the liquid should have evaporated.

three   Season well, and stir in the parsley just before serving.

Preparation time **5 minutes**   Cooking time **25 minutes**
Oven temperature **400°F**
Total time **30 minutes**   *Serves 4–6*

vegetable frittata

There are many variations of frittata. Usually they are made with vegetables, but try adding pancetta or chili salami.

one   Heat the olive oil in a skillet with a heat-proof handle. Add the onions, garlic, potatoes, red peppers, and zucchini, and sauté for 5 minutes.

two   Add the thyme, season with salt and pepper, and mix well. Pour in the beaten eggs and cook over moderate heat for 3 minutes.

three   Sprinkle with the grated Parmesan and put the pan in a preheated oven, 400°F, and cook for 15 minutes. The frittata should be set and golden on top.

four   Remove the pan from the oven, ease a knife all the way around the edge and under the frittata, slide it onto a large plate, and serve at once.

2 tablespoons olive oil
2 onions, finely sliced
2 garlic cloves, crushed and chopped
2 potatoes, boiled and sliced
2 red peppers, cored, deseeded, and cut into
strips
6 zucchini, sliced
1 thyme sprig, chopped
5 eggs, beaten
2 oz. Parmesan cheese, freshly grated
salt and pepper

Preparation time **5 minutes**   Cooking time **25 minutes**
Oven temperature **400°F**
Total time **30 minutes**
Serves 4–6

spinach and ricotta frittata

2 tablespoons olive oil
2 onions, finely sliced
5 eggs
1 garlic clove, crushed and chopped
1 lb. spinach, washed and chopped
6 oz. ricotta cheese
2 oz. pine nuts
1 oz. black olives, pitted and chopped
salt and pepper

one   Heat the olive oil in a skillet with a heat-proof handle, add the onions and garlic, and sauté for 3 minutes; do not brown.

two   Beat the eggs in a large bowl; season well with salt and pepper, then add the chopped spinach and crumble in three-quarters of the ricotta. Add the pine nuts and olives and mix well. Add the onions and garlic and mix again.

three   Heat a little more oil in the skillet, pour in the spinach mixture, and cook for 5 minutes.

four   Sprinkle with the remaining ricotta, season with salt and pepper, and place the pan in a preheated oven, 400°F, for 15 minutes.

five   When cooked, the frittata should be set and golden on top. To serve, ease a knife around the edge and underneath and slide the frittata onto a large plate. This dish can be eaten hot or cold.

Preparation time **5 minutes**
Cooking time **25 minutes**
Oven temperature **400°F**
Total time **30 minutes**
Serves 4

fennel baked with cream and Parmesan

1½ lb. fennel
small lump of butter
1 cup heavy cream
3 oz. freshly grated Parmesan cheese
salt and pepper

one   Trim the outside leaves from the fennel, remove the hard central core, and slice the fennel lengthwise. Immerse the leaves in a pan of boiling water and cook for 5 minutes. Drain well.

two   Butter a shallow ovenproof dish, add the fennel, and sprinkle with salt and pepper. Pour the cream over and sprinkle with the Parmesan.

three   Place the dish at the top of a preheated oven, 400°F, and cook for 20 minutes. Allow the top of the fennel to cook to a deep golden brown.

Preparation time **5 minutes**   Cooking time **25 minutes**
Oven temperature **425°F**
Total time **30 minutes**   *Serves 4*

roast vegetables with olive oil and chilies

4 tablespoons olive oil
8 oz. parsnips, cut into equal-size chunks
8 oz. leeks, cut into ½-inch lengths
8 oz. red peppers, cored, deseeded, and cut into squares
8 oz. eggplants, cut into chunks
½ teaspoon crushed dried chilies
handful of marjoram, chopped
salt and pepper

one   Place the olive oil in a large roasting pan and put it into a preheated oven, 425°F, for a few minutes to warm.

two   Add the parsnips to the pan, toss well in the oil, then return the pan to the top of the oven and cook the parsnips for 10 minutes.

three   Remove the pan from the oven and add the leeks, red peppers, eggplants, and crushed chilies. Toss to coat in the olive oil, then return the pan to the oven to cook for a further 15 minutes.

four   Remove the pan from the oven, add the chopped marjoram and salt and pepper to the vegetables; mix well and serve immediately.

Preparation time **5 minutes**   Cooking time **20 minutes**   Oven temperature **400°F**
Total time **25 minutes**   *Serves 4*

baked young celery with Parmesan

This recipe also works very well with fennel.

one   Butter a large ovenproof dish. Cut the celery heads into quarters lengthwise and place in the prepared dish. Add the oregano, drizzle with olive oil, and season well with salt and pepper.

two   Sprinkle the grated Parmesan over the celery and cook in a preheated oven, 400°F, for 20 minutes. The celery should become soft and the cheese golden and crunchy on top.

2 tablespoons butter
2 small young heads of celery
handful of oregano, chopped
3 tablespoons olive oil
3 oz. Parmesan cheese, freshly grated
salt and pepper

Preparation time **5 minutes**   Cooking time **25 minutes**
Oven temperature **375°F**   Total time **30 minutes**   *Serves 4*

baked eggplant and Gorgonzola

4 tablespoons olive oil
1 red onion, chopped
2 garlic cloves, crushed and
chopped
13 oz. can chopped tomatoes
1 red chili, diced
handful of basil, roughly torn
2 eggplants, thickly sliced
4 oz. Gorgonzola cheese
salt and pepper

one   Heat 1 tablespoon of the olive oil in a saucepan and sauté the onion and garlic for 3 minutes.

two   Add the tomatoes and chili and simmer for about 8–10 minutes until the sauce has reduced. Add the basil and season well with salt and pepper.

three   Heat the remaining olive oil in a large skillet, add the eggplant slices, and fry until golden on each side.

four   Place a layer of eggplants in a shallow ovenproof dish and spoon half of the sauce over. Make another layer of eggplants, then add the rest of the sauce, and finally crumble over the Gorgonzola. Bake in a preheated oven, 375°F, for 15 minutes.

Preparation time **5 minutes**   Cooking time **25 minutes**
Oven temperature **400°F**
Total time **30 minutes**   *Serves 4*

stuffed eggplants

2 eggplants
4 tablespoons olive oil
8 tomatoes, skinned and chopped
2 garlic cloves, crushed and
chopped
4 anchovy fillets, chopped
1 tablespoon capers, chopped
handful of basil, chopped
handful of flat-leafed parsley,
chopped
3 oz. pecorino cheese, grated
2 tablespoons pine nuts, toasted
(see opposite)
½ cup white breadcrumbs
salt and pepper

one   Cut the eggplants in half lengthwise and scoop out the flesh without breaking the skin. Coarsely chop the flesh.

two   Heat the olive oil in a skillet, add the eggplant shells, and sauté them on each side for 3–4 minutes. Place them in a lightly oiled baking dish and sauté the flesh until golden brown.

three   Mix together the chopped tomato, garlic, anchovies, capers, basil, parsley, half of the pecorino cheese, the pine nuts, breadcrumbs, and eggplant flesh and season with salt and pepper. Spoon the mixture into the sautéed eggplant shells, piling it high. Sprinkle with the remaining cheese, then place in a preheated oven, 400°F, and cook for 20 minutes.

These eggplants are delicious and can be served hot or cold. If you prefer, peppers and zucchini can be used instead.

Preparation time **5 minutes**   Cooking time **25 minutes**   Total time **30 minutes**   *Serves 4*

Sicilian eggplants

one   Heat the olive oil in a heavy-bottomed saucepan, add the onions, garlic, and celery, and sauté for 3 minutes.

two   Add the eggplant and yellow and red peppers, turn up the heat, and cook for a further 5 minutes, stirring constantly.

three   Add the tomato sauce and vinegar and bring to a boil, then reduce the heat so that the mixture just simmers for 10 minutes. Add the anchovies, capers, and olives, and simmer the mixture for a further 5 minutes.

four   Meanwhile, put the pine nuts into a heavy-bottomed pan and dry-fry until browned, stirring all the time as they cook very quickly.

five   Finally, season the eggplant mixture with pepper, add the pine nuts and chopped parsley, and mix well. Serve hot or at room temperature.

4 tablespoons olive oil
2 red onions, sliced
2 garlic cloves, crushed and
    chopped
2 celery stalks, chopped
1 eggplant, cut into small cubes
1 yellow pepper, cored, deseeded,
    and cut into thin strips
1 red pepper, cored, deseeded, and
    cut into thin strips
½ cup tomato sauce
2 tablespoons red wine vinegar
6 anchovy fillets, cut into long strips
2 oz. capers, coarsely chopped
4 oz. black olives, pitted
3 oz. pine nuts
handful of flat-leafed parsley,
    chopped
pepper

Preparation time **5 minutes**   Cooking time **10 minutes**
Total time **15 minutes**   *Serves 4*

broccoli with anchovies

3 oz. pine nuts
2 lbs. broccoli, cut
into florets
4 tablespoons butter
juice of 1 lemon
4 anchovy fillets, finely
chopped
3 oz. Parmesan
cheese, freshly
grated
salt and pepper

one   Place the pine nuts under a preheated broiler or in a heavy skillet and dry-fry until golden all over. Set aside.

two   Steam the broccoli or plunge it into boiling water for 2 minutes, then drain well and transfer to a bowl.

three   Melt the butter in a small saucepan, add the lemon juice and anchovies, and heat until the butter foams. Pour the melted butter over the broccoli, sprinkle with salt and pepper, and toss. To serve, top the broccoli with the Parmesan and pine nuts.

Preparation time **5 minutes**   Cooking time **20 minutes**
Oven temperature **400°F**
Total time **25 minutes**   *Serves 4*

potatoes wrapped in Parma ham

one   Roll each potato in a slice of Parma ham, patting with your hands to mold the ham to the shape of the potato.

two   Lightly oil a roasting pan, add the potatoes, and cook in a preheated oven, 400°F, for 20 minutes. Keep an eye on the potatoes while they are cooking as they may need turning, or moving around; often the ones on the edge get more color than the ones in the middle.

three   Serve the potatoes sprinkled with sea salt.

12 small new potatoes, cooked
12 very thin slices Parma ham
2 tablespoons olive oil
sea salt

Preparation time **5 minutes**   Cooking time **25 minutes**
Oven temperature **450°F**   Total time **30 minutes**   *Serves 4*

roast potatoes with rosemary and garlic

one   Cut the potatoes lengthwise into quarters, and make sure that they are dry.

two   Put 2 tablespoons of the olive oil into a large roasting pan, and place in a preheated oven, 450°F, to warm through.

three   Mix together the remaining oil and the rosemary and toss the potatoes to coat them completely.

four   Add the potatoes to the roasting pan in the oven, shake carefully to make an even layer, then place the pan at the top of the oven and roast for 20 minutes.

five   Remove the pan from the oven and move the potatoes around so that they cook evenly. Scatter the garlic among the potatoes, return the pan to the oven, and cook for a further 5 minutes. Remove the potatoes from the oven, season with salt and pepper, and serve immediately.

1½ lb. medium potatoes, unpeeled
4 tablespoons olive oil
2 tablespoons chopped rosemary
4 garlic cloves, peeled and sliced
salt and pepper

These potatoes are quite delicious and make an excellent accompaniment to fish, or can be served on their own as an appetizer. Alternatively, use very small potatoes and serve them with drinks.

Preparation time **5 minutes**   Cooking time **10 minutes**   Total time **15 minutes**   *Serves 4*

cavolo nero with pancetta

1 tablespoon olive oil
1 onion, sliced
1 garlic clove, crushed and chopped
1 red chili, cored, deseeded, and diced
4 oz. pancetta, diced
1 head cavolo nero
¼ cup plus 2 tablespoons chicken stock
3 oz. Parmesan cheese, coarsely grated
salt and pepper

one   Heat the olive oil in a large saucepan, add the onion, garlic, chili, and pancetta and sauté for 5 minutes or until soft.

two   To prepare the cavolo nero, trim any wilting leaves, then cut the heads in half lengthwise. Remove and discard the hard central stem and coarsely chop the leaves.

three   Add the cavolo nero to the onion mixture and stir well. Pour in the chicken stock and season with salt and pepper; cook for 4 minutes over moderate heat, stirring all the time.

four   Finally, add the grated Parmesan and serve at once.

Preparation time **5 minutes**   Cooking time **25 minutes**
Total time **30 minutes**   *Serves 4*

braised fava beans and lentils

2 tablespoons olive oil
1 red onion, chopped
2 garlic cloves, crushed and chopped
4 oz. pancetta or unsmoked bacon, diced
6 oz. puy lentils
2 lb. fresh or frozen fava beans
handful of marjoram, chopped
8 fresh or canned artichoke hearts, prepared
4 tablespoons butter
handful of flat-leafed parsley, chopped
salt and pepper

one   Heat the oil in a heavy-bottomed saucepan, add the onion, garlic, and pancetta, and sauté for 5 minutes.

two   Add the lentils, fava beans, marjoram, season with salt and pepper, and cover with hot water. Mix well and simmer for 15 minutes. The water may need to be topped up during cooking if the mixture is getting too thick and sticking to the bottom of the pan. Keep stirring, just to be sure that it does not stick.

three   Add the artichoke hearts and cook for 5 minutes. The mixture should be thick and rich. Finally, stir in the butter and parsley, taste for seasoning, and serve immediately.

Cavolo nero is an Italian cabbage with extremely long leaves, that is available in most of the larger supermarkets. It is almost the shape of a romaine lettuce, but the leaves are greenish purple in color. Cavolo nero has a simple cabbage-like flavor but a slightly firmer texture. Like all green cabbage, it is best not overcooked.

Fish and Shellfish

An abundance of fresh fish and shellfish is available in Italy. Charbroiling and simple cooking are the most popular methods of treating fresh fish.

Preparation time **5 minutes**   Cooking time **7 minutes**
Total time **12 minutes**   *Serves 4*

broiled sea bass

extra virgin olive oil
2 x 2 lb. sea bass, filleted
salt and pepper
2 lemons, halved, to serve

one   Lightly oil a baking sheet. Place
the 4 sea bass fillets on the baking sheet
and drizzle with olive oil. Season
generously with salt and pepper and
cook under a preheated very hot broiler
for 7 minutes. Serve with lemon halves
and Braised Fava Beans and Lentils (see
page 84).

Preparation time **10 minutes**
Cooking time **15 minutes**
Total time **25 minutes**   *Serves 4*

swordfish steaks in white wine and tomatoes

Choose a pan that the
pieces of fish will fit into as
neatly as possible: a skillet
may be best.

2 tablespoons olive oil
1 red onion, chopped
1 garlic clove, crushed and chopped
2 celery stalks, chopped
2 bay leaves
4 tomatoes, skinned and chopped
1 teaspoon sugar
¾ cup white wine
2 tablespoons chopped oregano
4 x 6 oz. swordfish steaks
salt and pepper

one   Heat the oil in a pan, add the onion, garlic, and
celery, and sauté gently for 5 minutes.

two   Add the bay leaves, tomatoes, sugar, white wine,
and oregano, season with salt and pepper, mix well, and
bring to a gentle simmer.

three   Add the swordfish steaks and cook for 5
minutes, then turn them over and cook on the other side
for a further 5 minutes. This dish can be served
immediately, or in hot weather it is very good at room
temperature.

Preparation time **15 minutes**   Cooking time **10 minutes**   Total time **25 minutes**   *Serves 4*

spicy fried sardines

Sardines must be fresh, bright eyed, with shiny fresh scales, and without an unpleasant smell. If you have any doubts, don't buy them. To gut the sardines, if the grocer hasn't done it for you, insert a knife in the belly, make a slit, and remove the contents. Cut off the heads just behind the gills and thoroughly wash the fish under cold running water. Drain and dry well.

oil, for deep-frying
1 cup all-purpose flour
1½ lb. large, fresh sardines
4 tablespoons olive oil
5 shallots, sliced
½ cup white wine vinegar
4 garlic cloves, crushed and chopped
large handful of mint leaves, finely chopped
rind and juice of 1 lemon
½ teaspoon crushed dried chilies
salt and pepper

one   Heat the oil for deep-frying. Season the flour with salt and pepper.

two   Dip the sardines into the seasoned flour and fry in the hot oil for 2 minutes or until golden. Remove and place on a tray lined with paper towels to absorb the excess oil. Keep warm.

three   Heat 1 tablespoon of the olive oil in a saucepan, add the shallots, and sauté for 5 minutes, then add the vinegar and cook until nearly half of it has evaporated.

four   Transfer the sardines to a warmed serving dish. Add the remaining olive oil, the garlic, mint, lemon rind and juice, and chilies to the onion mixture and cook for 1 minute. Spoon the sauce over the sardines and sprinkle with salt and pepper. This dish can be served hot or at room temperature.

Preparation time **5 minutes**   Cooking time **15 minutes**   Total time **20 minutes**   *Serves 4*

tuna steaks with sun-dried tomatoes

2 tablespoons olive oil
1 red onion, finely chopped
2 garlic cloves, crushed and chopped
1 rosemary sprig, chopped
¾ cup all-purpose flour
4 x 6 oz. tuna steaks, skinned
oil, for frying
4 oz. sun-dried tomatoes in oil, chopped
¼ cup plus 2 tablespoons red wine
1 tablespoon capers
3 oz. black olives
handful of flat-leafed parsley, chopped
salt and pepper
1 lemon, cut into 4 wedges, to serve

one   Heat the olive oil in a saucepan, add the onion, garlic, and rosemary, and sauté gently for 5 minutes.

two   Season the flour with salt and pepper. Dip the tuna steaks into the seasoned flour to coat evenly all over.

three   Heat the oil in a skillet, add the tuna steaks, and cook for 4–5 minutes until golden. Turn over and cook on the other side for a further 4–5 minutes. Transfer the tuna steaks to a dish lined with paper towels and keep warm in the oven.

four   Add the sun-dried tomatoes to the sautéed onions and stir well. Turn up the heat to high, add the red wine, capers, olives, parsley, season with salt and pepper, and simmer for 2 minutes. Serve the sauce with the tuna steaks and wedges of lemon.

Preparation time **10 minutes**
Cooking time **15 minutes**
Total time **25 minutes**
Serves 4

broiled red mullet with salsa verde

4 x 12 oz. red mullet, scaled and
cleaned
Salsa verde:
4 oz. parsley, chopped
4 oz. basil, chopped
5 anchovy fillets, coarsely chopped
2 tablespoons capers
2 garlic cloves, crushed and
chopped
juice and rind of 1 lemon
½ cup olive oil
salt and pepper

one   Make 3 slashes across the fish on each side and season with salt and pepper. Place under a preheated very hot broiler and cook on each side for 6–8 minutes, or until cooked.

two   To make the salsa verde, put the parsley, basil, anchovies, capers, and garlic into a food processor or blender and blend to a smooth paste. Add the lemon juice and rind and olive oil; season with salt and pepper and blend again.

three   Remove the fish from the broiler and put a spoonful of the salsa verde into each of the slashes on one side of the fish. Serve the remaining salsa at the table in a small dish.

trout with Parmesan and basil dressing

Preparation time **10 minutes**
Cooking time **10 minutes**
Total time **20 minutes**
Serves 4

4 tablespoons olive oil
4 x 7 oz. trout fillets
large handful of basil leaves, coarsely chopped
1 garlic clove, crushed and chopped
4 oz. Parmesan cheese, freshly grated
salt and pepper

one   Lightly brush a baking sheet with oil and place under a preheated very hot broiler to heat up.

two   Put the trout fillets onto the hot baking sheet, sprinkle with salt and pepper, and place under the broiler for 5 minutes.

three   Put the basil and garlic into a bowl. Work in the olive oil using a hand-held mixer.

four   Remove the fish from the broiler and sprinkle with the grated Parmesan. Return to the broiler and cook for a further 3–5 minutes, until the Parmesan turns golden. Serve with the basil sauce drizzled over the golden trout fillets.

Salsa verde, literally translated as green sauce, is traditionally served with "bollito mista," a north Italian dish of boiled meats and poultry. It also tastes great on fresh bread.

Preparation time **10 minutes**   Cooking time **15 minutes**   Total time **25 minutes**   *Serves 4*

fish casserole

3 tablespoons olive oil
2 red onions, finely diced
2 garlic cloves, crushed and chopped
½ teaspoon crushed dried chilies
7 oz. squid, cleaned and cut into thin lengths
7 oz. mussels, scrubbed and debearded
7 oz. clams, cleaned (see page 32)
10 oz. raw tiger shrimp in their shells
150 ml/¼ pint fish stock
½ cup dry white wine
½ teaspoon saffron
8 tomatoes, skinned and deseeded
1 bay leaf
1 teaspoon sugar
1 lb. red mullet fillets, cut into bite-sized pieces
handful of flat-leafed parsley, chopped salt and pepper

one   Heat the oil in a large saucepan—large enough to hold all the ingredients. Add the onion and garlic and sauté gently for 5 minutes, then add the chilies and mix well.

two   Add the squid, mussels, clams, and tiger shrimp and stir well.

three   Add the fish stock, wine, saffron, tomatoes, bay leaf, and sugar and season with salt and pepper. Cover the pan and simmer gently for 5 minutes. Discard any mussels or clams that do not open.

four   Add the red mullet, sprinkle with the parsley, and simmer for a further 5 minutes, then serve immediately. This is a very simple dish to make but finger bowls are needed at the table as it is very messy to eat. Serve with Bruschetta (see page 20) and a green salad.

Preparation time **5 minutes**   Cooking time **25 minutes**
Oven temperature **425°F**
Total time **30 minutes**   *Serves 4*

baked cod with potatoes and olives

pat of butter
12 oz. potatoes, thinly sliced
thyme sprig, separated into leaves
4 x 7 oz. cod fillets
2 tablespoons pitted black olives
2 tablespoons olive oil
salt and pepper

one   Rub the butter over a shallow ovenproof dish.

two   Arrange the potatoes in layers in the buttered dish, sprinkling each layer with a little thyme and salt and pepper

three   Place the pieces of cod on top of the potatoes, add the olives, drizzle with olive oil, season with salt and pepper, and add a little thyme. Put the dish in the middle of a preheated oven, 425°F, and cook for 25 minutes. Check to be sure that the potatoes are soft before serving.

Preparation time **5 minutes**   Cooking time **25 minutes**   Oven temperature 400°F
Total time **30 minutes**   *Serves 4*

halibut in paper packets

one   Cut 4 sheets of waxed paper large enough to enclose the fish and vegetables.

two   To prepare the fennel, trim the top and outer leaves, remove the hard central core, and cut the bulb into slices through the root. Divide evenly among the sheets of waxed paper and put the fish on top. Sprinkle with the shallots, olives, and sage, season with salt and pepper, and finish with a slice of lemon. The waxed paper can be folded over and rolled at the edges to seal, but a much easier way is to fold the paper and staple it. Put the packets onto a baking sheet, and cook in a preheated oven, 400°F, for 25 minutes.

three   Serve these packets at the table so that everyone opens their own packet and gets a waft of the delicious aroma that escapes when they are first opened.

1 fennel bulb
4 x 7 oz. halibut fillets
2 shallots, finely chopped
8 pitted black olives
a few sage leaves, torn
4 lemon slices
salt and pepper

Preparation time **10 minutes**   Cooking time **15 minutes**
Oven temperature **425°F**
Total time **25 minutes**   *Serves 4*

roast monkfish with Parma ham

4 x 6 oz. monkfish fillets
4 rosemary sprigs
8 slices Parma ham
2 tablespoons olive oil
1 red onion, chopped
1 garlic clove, crushed and chopped
6 tomatoes, skinned, deseeded and coarsely chopped
1 teaspoon capers, coarsely chopped
handful of flat-leafed parsley
salt and pepper

one   Season the monkfish with salt and pepper, place the rosemary sprigs on the fish, and wrap the slices of Parma ham around them. Put the fish in a lightly oiled baking dish and cook in a preheated oven, 425°F, for 15 minutes.

two   Heat 1 tablespoon of the oil in a saucepan, add the onion and garlic, and sauté gently for 5 minutes.

three   Add the tomatoes and capers, mix well, then add the remaining olive oil and parsley and season with salt and pepper.

four   Serve the fish with some of the sauce spooned over one end.

Preparation time **5 minutes**   Cooking time **25 minutes**   Oven temperature 450°F
Total time **30 minutes**   *Serves 4*

roast cod with vegetables

1½ lb. cod fillets, skinned
4 potatoes, unpeeled and quartered
6 tomatoes, halved
1 red onion, quartered
1 fennel bulb, cut into wedges
2 garlic cloves, crushed and chopped
3 oz. black olives, pitted
1 oz. green olives, pitted
1 oz. capers
juice of 1 lemon
3 tablespoons olive oil
salt and pepper
handful of parsley, chopped, to garnish

one   Put the cod, potatoes, tomatoes, onion, and fennel into a large lightly oiled dish. Try to arrange them in a single layer. Sprinkle with the olives, capers, and lemon juice, and season with salt and pepper.

two   Drizzle with olive oil and place in the top of a preheated oven, 450°F, and roast for 25 minutes.

three   Garnish with flat-leafed parsley and serve with warm focaccia bread.

Preparation time **5 minutes**   Cooking time **25 minutes**
Oven temperature 400°F   Total time **30 minutes**   *Serves 4*

mussels with fresh tomato and pepper sauce

1 red pepper
2 tablespoons olive oil
2 red onions, chopped
2 garlic cloves, crushed and chopped
6 tomatoes, peeled and chopped
½ teaspoon crushed dried chili
½ cup dry white wine
2 lb. mussels, scrubbed and debearded
2 tablespoons capers
large handful of flat-leafed parsley, coarsely chopped
salt and pepper

one   To skin the red pepper, first cut off the bottom of the pepper. Put the pepper on a chopping board and slice off 4–5 flat pieces, leaving the seeds and core intact. Place the pepper pieces under a hot broiler and broil until the skins blister and blacken, then peel off the skins and coarsely chop the flesh.

two   Heat the oil in a large ovenproof casserole, add the onions and garlic, and sauté for 5 minutes. Do not brown.

three   Add the tomatoes, chili, and white wine and simmer for 5 minutes to reduce and thicken the sauce.

four   Add the mussels and capers and season with salt and pepper. Mix well, cover with a lid, and bake in a preheated oven, 400°F, for 8 minutes.

five   Remove the casserole from the oven. Check the mussels and discard any that have not opened. Stir in the parsley and serve with warm focaccia bread.

Preparation time **15 minutes**   Cooking time **6 minutes**   Total time **21 minutes**   *Serves 4*

pan-fried squid with chilies

2 lb. small squid, cleaned
2 tablespoons olive oil
3 garlic cloves, crushed and chopped
1 red chili, finely chopped
juice of 1 lemon
handful of flat-leafed parsley, chopped
salt and pepper

one   Slit the squid down one side and lay them flat. Score the skin of each one with a fine criss-cross pattern.

two   Mix the olive oil, garlic, chili, and lemon juice in a bowl and add the squid. Mix well to coat all over, cover, and marinate for 15 minutes.

three   Remove the squid from the marinade, reserving the marinade. Heat a large skillet or a wok with 2 tablespoons of oil until it is just smoking. Add the squid, season with salt and pepper, stir well, and cook over high heat for 2–3 minutes. The squid will curl up, but just hold them flat for a few seconds to get a tasty browned outside. Finally add the strained marinade and the parsley to the pan, mix well, and serve at once.

Preparation time **5 minutes**   Cooking time **6 minutes**   Total time **11 minutes**   *Serves 4*

tiger shrimp with garlic and herbs

4 tablespoons butter
2 tablespoons olive oil
1½ lb. peeled raw tiger shrimp
1 shallot, finely diced
2 garlic cloves, crushed and chopped
¼ cup plus 2 tablespoons dry white wine
4 oz. flat-leafed parsley, chopped
4 oz. marjoram, chopped
salt and pepper

This dish goes very well with egg pasta, or it can be served on its own with warm ciabatta bread to mop up all the juices.

one   Melt the butter with the oil in a skillet, add the tiger shrimp, shallot, and garlic, and sauté for 5 minutes or until all the shrimp have turned pink.

two   Add the white wine, parsley, and marjoram, and season with salt and pepper. Mix well and serve immediately.

Preparation time **10 minutes**   Cooking time **5 minutes**   Total time **15 minutes**   *Serves 4*

seared scallops with basil and balsamic vinegar

16 large scallops, cleaned
3 tablespoons olive oil
2 shallots, finely chopped
4 tablespoons balsamic vinegar
large handful of basil leaves, torn
salt and pepper

one   Check that the scallops are clean; there should be no wet brown patches. If there are, trim them off, leaving the white meat and orange coral.

two   Heat the oil in a large skillet over high heat until it is just smoking, then add the scallops and cook for 2 minutes on one side. Turn them over and add the shallots. Cook for 1 minute, then reduce the heat. Add the balsamic vinegar and season with salt and pepper, then turn the scallops to coat in the vinegar.

three   Sprinkle the basil over the scallops, quickly mix, and serve immediately.

Chop the squid tentacles and use them in this dish as they look very pretty. Their faint purple color is subtly complemented by the red chili.

Poultry, Game, and Meat

High-quality meat and game are available throughout Italy, so often all that is needed is brief cooking and a sprinkling of olive oil, salt, and black pepper. Older cuts are simmered in rich wine sauces to produce wonderfully tender dishes.

Preparation time **10 minutes**   Cooking time **20 minutes**
Total time **30 minutes**   *Serves 4*

country chicken

4 tablespoons butter
2 tablespoons olive oil
4 boneless chicken breasts
1 onion, chopped
½ small celery head, chopped
1 garlic clove, crushed and chopped
½ teaspoon crushed dried chili
1 cup tomato sauce
1 bay leaf
thyme sprig
handful of oregano, coarsely chopped
salt and pepper

one   Melt the butter with the oil in a skillet. When it is hot, add the chicken breasts and cook on each side for about 5 minutes. Let them brown as this adds to the flavor of the sauce.

two   Remove the chicken with a slotted spoon and set aside. Add the onion, celery, garlic, and chili to the pan and sauté for 5 minutes.

three   Add the tomato sauce, bay leaf, and thyme. Season with salt and pepper and stir well. Return the chicken breasts to the sauce and simmer for 10 minutes. Just before serving add the coarsely chopped oregano.

chicken with wild mushrooms

Preparation time **5 minutes**
Cooking time **25 minutes**
Total time **30 minutes**   *Serves 4*

2 oz. dried wild mushrooms, soaked, or 8 oz. fresh mushrooms, sliced
½ cup all-purpose flour
4 skinless, boneless chicken breasts
4 tablespoons butter
1 tablespoon olive oil
2 shallots, diced
2 garlic cloves, crushed and chopped
½ cup white wine
4 oz. mascarpone cheese
handful of chives, snipped
salt and pepper

one   If using dried mushrooms, put them into a bowl and just cover with hot water. Soak for 15 minutes.

two   Meanwhile, season the flour with salt and pepper and toss the chicken in the seasoned flour to cover all over.

three   Heat the butter and oil in a skillet, add the chicken, and cook on each side for 4 minutes or until colored. Remove the chicken and keep warm.

four   Add the shallots and garlic to the pan and sauté gently for 5 minutes. Add the wine and mix well to include any tasty brown bits from the pan.

five   Add the mascarpone and the mushrooms to the pan; if using wild mushrooms, add the soaking liquid. Mix well to melt the mascarpone. If the mixture is very runny, turn up the heat to evaporate some of the liquid. If you are using fresh mushrooms, add a little extra liquid, but mushrooms make their own liquid as they cook.

six   Return the chicken to the pan and simmer gently for 10 minutes, turning it from time to time. Finally, stir the chives into the pan and serve immediately.

Preparation time **5 minutes**
Cooking time **25 minutes**
Total time **30 minutes**
Serves 4

Roman chicken

4 tablespoons olive oil
2 red onions, sliced
2 garlic cloves, sliced
2 red peppers, cored, deseeded, and sliced
2 yellow peppers, cored, deseeded, and sliced
½ teaspoon crushed dried chilies
8 boneless chicken thighs
½ cup white wine
large handful of basil, roughly torn
salt and pepper

one   Heat the olive oil in a large skillet, add the onions, garlic, red and yellow peppers, and chilies, and sauté for 5 minutes.

two   Add the chicken thighs, pushing them down to the bottom of the pan to seal on the outside. Cook for a further 5 minutes.

three   Add the wine and salt and pepper to taste, cover the pan, and cook for about 15 minutes over low heat. Check occasionally that the chicken and sauce do not stick to the bottom of the pan, and add a little more wine, if necessary.

four   Stir in the basil just before serving.

Preparation time **5 minutes, plus marinating**   Cooking time **15 minutes**
Total time **25 minutes**   *Serves 4*

chicken with rosemary and garlic

2 tablespoons olive oil
2 tablespoons white wine vinegar
2 tablespoons chopped rosemary
3 garlic cloves, crushed and chopped
1 teaspoon paprika
pared rind of 1 lemon
4 boneless, skinless chicken breasts, cut into long thin strips
handful of flat-leafed parsley, chopped
salt and pepper

one   Mix together the olive oil, vinegar, rosemary, garlic, paprika, and lemon rind in a bowl and season with salt and pepper. Add the chicken and mix well, then marinate for 10 minutes. Alternatively, this could be done the night before.

two   Heat a large nonstick pan, add the chicken and the marinade, mix well, and cook over moderate heat, stirring constantly, for 15 minutes.

three   To serve, stir in the chopped parsley.

Preparation time **10 minutes**   Cooking time **20 minutes**
Oven temperature **400°F**   Total time **30 minutes**   *Serves 4*

black olive chicken rolls

3 garlic cloves, crushed and chopped
2 tablespoons capers
4 anchovy fillets, chopped
1 teaspoon thyme leaves
1 shallot, chopped
6 oz. pitted black olives
1 tablespoon olive oil
4 small boneless, skinless chicken breasts
salt and pepper

one   Put the garlic, capers, anchovies, thyme, shallot, olives, and olive oil into a food processor or blender and blend together.

two   Place each chicken breast between 2 sheets of waxed paper and flatten to about 2½ times its original size by pounding with a rolling pin. Season the chicken breasts with salt and pepper and spread each one with a thin layer of the olive paste.

three   Roll up the breasts and secure with 2 toothpicks. Cut each chicken roll in half and place in a lightly oiled ovenproof dish. Cover with foil and cook in the top of a preheated oven, 400°F, for 20 minutes or until cooked. Serve with pasta tossed in olive oil, parsley, and Parmesan.

Preparation time **5 minutes**   Cooking time **25 minutes**
Oven temperature **400°F**
Total time **30 minutes**   *Serves 4*

chicken stuffed with spinach and ricotta

4 boneless, skinless chicken breasts
4 oz. ricotta cheese
4 oz. cooked spinach, squeezed dry
¼ teaspoon grated nutmeg
8 slices Parma ham
2 tablespoons olive oil
salt and pepper

one   Make a long horizontal slit through the thickness of each chicken breast without cutting all the way through.

two   Crumble the ricotta into a bowl. Chop the spinach and add to the ricotta with the nutmeg. Season with salt and pepper and mix well.

three   Divide the stuffing between the 4 chicken breasts and wrap each one in 2 pieces of Parma ham, winding it around the chicken to totally cover the meat.

four   Heat the oil in a shallow ovenproof pan, add the chicken breasts, and sauté for 4 minutes on each side or until the ham starts to brown. Transfer the pan to a preheated oven, 400°F, and cook for 15 minutes. The ham should be browned and slightly crunchy on the outside and the chicken moist and soft.

Preparation time **10 minutes**
Cooking time **20 minutes**
Total time **30 minutes** *Serves 4*

rolled stuffed chicken breasts

4 boneless, skinless chicken breasts
4 slices Parma ham
4 thin slices buffalo mozzarella
4 asparagus tips
¾ cup all-purpose flour
1 tablespoon olive oil
4 tablespoons butter
¼ cup dry white wine
¼ cup plus 2 tablespoons chicken stock
salt and pepper

one   Place each chicken breast between 2 sheets of waxed paper and flatten to about 2½ times its original size by pounding with a rolling pin.

two   Season the chicken with salt and pepper, place a slice of Parma ham, a slice of mozzarella, and an asparagus tip on top, and tightly roll up the chicken scallops. Tie with a piece of string or spear with toothpicks.

three   Season the flour with salt and pepper. Dip the prepared chicken rolls in the flour, coating them evenly all over.

four   Heat the olive oil and half of the butter in a skillet, add the chicken rolls, and sauté over low heat for 15 minutes or until golden all over, turning frequently to brown the chicken evenly.

five   Remove the chicken, place in a warmed serving dish, and keep warm. Pour the wine and chicken stock into the pan, bring to a boil, and simmer for 3 minutes.

six   Remove the string or toothpicks just before serving the chicken. Add the remaining butter to the pan, mix quickly with a small whisk to emulsify the sauce, then spoon over the chicken and serve with steamed asparagus.

Preparation time **5 minutes**
Cooking time **10 minutes**
Total time **15 minutes** *Serves 4*

chicken livers with Marsala and oregano

6 tablespoons butter
2 oz. pancetta or bacon, diced
1 shallot, diced
1 garlic clove, crushed and chopped
1 lb. chicken livers, trimmed
¾ cup Marsala
1 tablespoon chopped oregano
salt and pepper

one   Melt half of the butter in a large skillet, add the pancetta, shallot, and garlic, and sauté for 5 minutes without allowing to color, then remove from the pan.

two   Melt the remaining butter, add the chicken livers, and cook over high heat for 3 minutes until the chicken livers are evenly brown on the outside. Chicken livers are best when browned on the outside but still pink in the middle.

three   Return the shallot mixture to the pan and mix well. Add the Marsala and oregano and season with salt and pepper. Bring quickly to a boil. Serve immediately with buttered tagliatelle.

Preparation time **5 minutes**   Cooking time **25 minutes**   Total time **30 minutes**   *Serves 4*

duck breasts with balsamic vinegar

one   Heat the oil in a skillet, add the duck breasts, skin side down, and cook over moderate heat for 5 minutes, then reduce the heat and cook for another 10 minutes. Drain the excess oil from the duck skin.

two   Turn the duck breasts over and add the balsamic vinegar along with the cranberries and sugar. Season with salt and pepper and cook for a further 10 minutes.

three   Serve the duck breast with the sauce spooned over. The cranberries will have broken down and made a delicious sauce with the vinegar and duck juices, and the duck breasts should be pink and juicy in the middle.

1 tablespoon oil
4 boneless duck breasts
4 tablespoons balsamic vinegar
3 oz. cranberries
¼ cup brown sugar
salt and pepper

Preparation time **10 minutes**   Cooking time **20 minutes**
Total time **30 minutes**   *Serves 4*

broiled chicken with fresh herb sauce

4 boneless chicken breasts
2 tablespoons olive oil
salt and pepper
Herb sauce:
3 garlic cloves, crushed and chopped
4 anchovy fillets, chopped
large handful of flat-leafed parsley
handful of arugula leaves
handful of sorrel leaves
handful of basil leaves
juice of ½ lemon
½ cup extra virgin olive oil

one   Put the chicken breasts, skin side up, on a lightly oiled broiler pan, brush with a little olive oil, and season with salt and pepper. Place the pan under a preheated hot broiler and cook the chicken for about 10 minutes on each side.

two   Meanwhile, make the herb sauce. Put the garlic, anchovies, parsley, arugula, sorrel, basil, and lemon juice in a food processor or blender and blend for 1 minute. With the motor running, slowly drizzle in the olive oil; the sauce should be thick and bright green, with a strong fresh aroma. Finally, season with salt and pepper and blend again.

three   The chicken is ready when the skin is crunchy and dark brown. Serve with a little herb sauce on each plate and the rest at the table in a small dish.

This herb sauce is best eaten the day it is made, but can be kept for 1 day; it just loses its fresh aroma and bright green color.

braised breast of wood pigeon

¾ cup all-purpose flour
8 wood pigeon breasts, skinned
2 tablespoons olive oil
1 red onion, chopped
2 garlic cloves, crushed and chopped
3 celery stalks, chopped
1 cup red wine
grated rind of 1 orange
thyme sprig
rosemary sprig
1 bay leaf
½ teaspoon ground cinnamon
2 teaspoons juniper berries, crushed
¾ cup plus 2 tablespoons currant jelly
handful of flat-leafed parsley, chopped
salt and pepper

one   Season the flour with salt and pepper. Dip the wood pigeon breasts into the seasoned flour and coat evenly.

two   Heat the oil in a wide saucepan, add the pigeon breasts, and cook for 2 minutes on each side. Remove from the pan.

three   Add the onion, garlic, and celery, and sauté for 5 minutes. Increase the heat and pour in the red wine, stirring well to incorporate any tasty brown bits from the pan.

four   Add the orange rind, thyme, rosemary, bay leaf, cinnamon, juniper berries, currant jelly, and season with salt and pepper. Return the pigeon breasts to the pan and baste well with the sauce. Simmer for 10 minutes.

five   Remove the pigeon from the pan and keep warm. Increase the heat and reduce the liquid to make a rich glaze for the pigeon. Return the pigeon breasts to the pan, add the parsley, and serve.

quail with artichoke hearts

¾ cup all-purpose flour
4 prepared quails, weighing 8 oz. each
2 tablespoons olive oil
1 onion, chopped
2 celery stalks, chopped
2 garlic cloves, peeled and crushed
1 cup white wine
handful of sage, chopped
13 oz. jar prepared artichoke hearts
salt and pepper

one   Sprinkle the flour on a plate and season with salt and pepper. Dip the quail in the seasoned flour, coating them evenly.

two   Heat the oil in a large saucepan, add the quail, and brown all over. Remove from the pan and keep warm.

three   Add the onion, celery, and garlic, and sauté for 3 minutes, then pour in the wine, scraping any browned bits from the bottom of the pan.

four   Return the quail to the pan with the sage and artichoke hearts and season well. Cover the pan and simmer for 20 minutes, turning the quail from time to time. Serve with fresh pasta tossed in butter.

This dish is very good made the night before and left for all the flavors to mingle. When buying the quails, ask the butcher to take off the skin, cut the quails in half, and remove the spine from each bird.

Serve the rabbit on a bed of
pappardelle, if desired.
Pappardelle is the traditional
pasta to be served with game.

Preparation time **5 minutes**   Cooking time **25 minutes**
Total time **30 minutes**   *Serves 4*

pan-cooked
rabbit with sage

2 tablespoons olive oil
1 rabbit, cut into 8 pieces
handful of chopped sage
1 large rosemary sprig
½ cup dry white wine
1 tablespoon Dijon mustard
salt and pepper
handful of flat-leafed parsley,
chopped, to serve

one   Heat the oil in a large skillet, add the rabbit pieces, and brown all over.

two   Season well with salt and pepper. Add the sage, rosemary, wine, and mustard, mix thoroughly, and coat the rabbit in the wine sauce.

three   Simmer the rabbit for 20 minutes, turning frequently so that it cooks evenly.

four   To serve, sprinkle the rabbit pieces generously with the coarsely chopped parsley.

Preparation time **5 minutes**   Cooking time **25 minutes**
Total time **30 minutes**   *Serves 4*

sweet and
sour rabbit

¾ cup all-purpose flour
1 rabbit, cut into 8 pieces
2 tablespoons olive oil
1 onion, diced
1 garlic clove, crushed and chopped
1 cup red wine
rosemary sprig
4 tablespoons balsamic vinegar
1 tablespoon brown sugar
2 tablespoons golden raisins
2 tablespoons pine nuts, toasted
2 tablespoons black olives, pitted and
coarsely chopped
salt and pepper

one   Season the flour with the salt and pepper. Coat the rabbit evenly all over in the seasoned flour.

two   Heat the olive oil in a large skillet; add the rabbit pieces, turning to brown them all over, then remove with a slotted spoon and set aside.

three   Add the onion and garlic and sauté for 5 minutes; do not brown, just soften.

four   Return the rabbit to the pan, pour in the red wine, and add the rosemary, vinegar, sugar, golden raisins, and season with salt and pepper. Simmer for 20 minutes, turning the rabbit to coat it in the sauce and cook evenly.

five   Just before serving, add the pine nuts and olives, and stir to mix well.

Preparation time **10 minutes**
Cooking time **15 minutes**
Total time **25 minutes**   *Serves 4*

broiled fillet of venison

4 x 6 oz. venison steaks
2 tablespoons olive oil
1 shallot, finely chopped
2 garlic cloves, crushed and chopped
1 cup red wine
4 cloves
1 piece cinnamon stick
pared rind of 1 orange
10 juniper berries, crushed
3 tablespoons currant jelly
salt and pepper

one   Brush the venison steaks with the olive oil and season well with salt and pepper.

two   Heat a little oil in a saucepan, add the shallot and garlic, and sauté for 3 minutes. Add the wine, cloves, cinnamon, orange rind, juniper berries, and currant jelly, and simmer until it reduces to a rich sauce.

three   While the sauce is cooking, place the venison steaks on a broiler rack and cook under a preheated hot broiler for 6 minutes on each side.

four   To serve, strain the sauce and spoon over the venison steaks. Serve with pasta tossed in butter or Creamed Polenta with Dolcelatte and Mascarpone (see page 54).

Preparation time **5 minutes**   Cooking time **25 minutes**
Oven temperature **450°F**
Total time **30 minutes**   *Serves 4*

roast pork fillet with rosemary and fennel

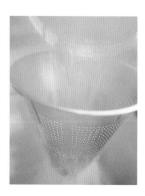

1 large rosemary sprig
3 garlic cloves
1½ lb. pork fillet, trimmed
4 tablespoons olive oil
2 fennel bulbs, trimmed and cut into wedges, central core removed
½ cup white wine
3 oz. mascarpone cheese
salt and pepper
rosemary sprigs, to garnish

one   Break the rosemary into short pieces and cut the garlic into slices. Pierce the pork with a sharp knife and insert the pieces of rosemary and garlic evenly all over the fillet.

two   Heat 2 tablespoons of the olive oil in a skillet, add the pork fillet, and fry for 5 minutes or until browned all over.

three   Lightly oil a roasting pan, add the fennel, and drizzle with olive oil. Place the pork fillet on top, season generously, and roast in a preheated oven, 450°F, for 20 minutes.

four   Pour the wine into the skillet and simmer until reduced by half. Add the mascarpone and season with salt and pepper. Stir to mix well.

five   To serve, cut the pork into slices and arrange on a warmed serving dish with wedges of fennel. Pour the sauce into the roasting pan and place on the heat. Using a wooden spoon, stir all the tasty bits into the sauce, then spoon over the pork and fennel. Garnish with rosemary.

Preparation time **5 minutes, plus marinating**
Cooking time **10 minutes**   Total time **15 minutes**   *Serves 4*

lamb chops with rosemary and lemon

1 rosemary sprig, finely chopped
1 tablespoon olive oil
rind and juice of 1 lemon
8 lamb cutlets
salt and pepper

It is important that the broiler is very hot for this recipe. It seals the meat quickly and browns the outside, leaving the inside pink.

one   Mix the rosemary, olive oil, and lemon rind and juice in a shallow dish, and season with salt and pepper. Add the lamb cutlets and coat with the marinade. Marinate for 10 minutes.

two   Place the chops on a broiler pan and spoon the marinade over. Place under a preheated very hot broiler and cook for 5 minutes on each side. Serve with Creamed Polenta with Dolcelatte and Mascarpone (see page 54).

Thin green beans simply cooked in boiling water for 2 minutes complement this rich and tasty dish.

Preparation time **10 minutes**   Cooking time **10 minutes**   Total time **20 minutes**   *Serves 4*

Parmesan breaded lamb chops

¾ cup all-purpose flour
8 lamb chops, trimmed
2 oz. Parmesan cheese, freshly grated
2 oz. fresh breadcrumbs
2 eggs, beaten
2 tablespoons olive oil
salt and pepper
1 lemon, cut into 4 wedges, to serve

one   Season the flour with salt and pepper. Dip the lamb chops into the seasoned flour, coating them evenly all over. Mix together the Parmesan and breadcrumbs and season with salt and pepper.

two   Dip the cutlets first in the beaten egg and then in the Parmesan mixture and coat all over, pressing the crumbs onto the lamb.

three   Heat the oil in a skillet, add the lamb chops, and cook on each side for 4 minutes or until golden. Be careful when turning them over; a thin spatula is best, so as not to loosen any of the cheesy crust from the chops.

four   Serve immediately with lemon wedges.

Preparation time **10 minutes**   Cooking time **8 minutes**
Total time **18 minutes**   *Serves 4*

fillet steak wrapped in Parma ham

handful of chopped marjoram
2 garlic cloves, crushed and finely chopped
4 x 6 oz. fillet steaks
8 slices Parma ham
4 oz. buffalo mozzarella, cut into 4 slices
salt and pepper

one   Mix together the marjoram and garlic and season with salt and pepper. Coat the steaks with the herb mixture, then wrap them in the Parma ham. Make sure that all the steak is covered with the ham.

two   Put the steaks on a greased broiler rack and place under a preheated very hot broiler, as close to the heat as possible without burning them. Cook on each side for 3 minutes if you like your steak rare, 5–6 minutes for medium, and 8 minutes for well done.

three   Place the slices of mozzarella on the steaks, return to the broiler, and cook until the mozzarella is melting and just turning golden.

four   Remove the steaks from the broiler and let stand for 5 minutes before serving. This allows the meat to relax.

Preparation time **10 minutes**   Cooking time **10 minutes**   Total time **20 minutes**   *Serves 4*

breaded veal scallops with Parma ham and Parmesan

one   Place the veal scallops between 2 sheets of waxed paper and flatten them by pounding with a rolling pin or meat mallet.

two   Season the flour with salt and pepper. Dip the scallops first in the flour, then in the egg, and finally in the breadcrumbs, coating them evenly.

three   Melt the butter in a large skillet. When it is foaming, add the scallops and cook on each side for 1–2 minutes or until golden.

four   Place the scallops on a broiler pan. Put a piece of Parma ham on each one and sprinkle with grated Parmesan. Place the scallops under a preheated very hot broiler and cook for 4–5 minutes until the Parmesan is golden.

five   Garnish the scallops with chopped parsley and serve with lemon wedges.

4 x 6 oz. veal scallops
¾ cup all-purpose flour
2 eggs, beaten
¾ cup fresh breadcrumbs
6 tablespoons butter
2 oz. Parma ham
2 oz. Parmesan cheese, freshly grated
salt and pepper
handful of flat-leafed parsley, chopped, to garnish
1 lemon, cut into 4 wedges, to serve

Preparation time **10 minutes**
Cooking time **10 minutes**
Total time **20 minutes**
Serves 4

veal scallops with lemon and pine nuts

¾ cup all-purpose flour
4 x 6 oz. veal scallops
4 tablespoons butter
1 tablespoon olive oil
3 oz. pine nuts
rind and juice of 1 lemon
¼ cup plus 2 tablespoons chicken stock
handful of parsley, finely chopped
salt and pepper

one   Season the flour with salt and pepper. Dip the scallops into the seasoned flour, coating them evenly all over.

two   Heat the butter and oil in a skillet. When it is foaming, add the scallops and cook on each side for about 3 minutes until golden.

three   Sprinkle the pine nuts into the pan and stir until golden.

four   Add the lemon rind and juice, chicken stock, and parsley, and season with salt and pepper. Bring to a boil and mix well. Serve immediately with Risotto alla Milanese (see page 40).

It is important that all the ingredients for the gremolata
are finely chopped or grated, as they mix together
better, making a more subtle blend.

Preparation time **5 minutes**　Cooking time **25 minutes**
Oven temperature **400°F**　Total time **30 minutes**　*Serves 4*

veal chops with gremolata

4 thin veal chops
¾ cup seasoned flour
4 tablespoons butter
1 tablespoon olive oil
2 onions, chopped
2 garlic cloves, crushed and chopped
2 celery stalks, chopped
1 carrot, chopped
2 bay leaves
6 tomatoes, skinned, deseeded, and chopped
½ cup chicken stock
½ cup dry white wine
salt and pepper
Gremolata:
2 tablespoons finely chopped parsley
1 tablespoon finely chopped sage
rind of 3 lemons, finely grated
3 large garlic cloves, crushed and chopped

one　Coat both sides of the veal chops with seasoned flour. Melt the butter and oil in a flameproof casserole, add the chops, and brown well on each side. Remove from the casserole and keep warm.

two　Add the onions, garlic, celery, and carrot to the pan and sauté for 3 minutes.

three　Add the bay leaves, tomatoes, stock, wine, and salt and pepper, mix well, and bring to a boil. Return the chops to the casserole and turn to coat them in the sauce. Cover and cook in a preheated oven, 400°F, for 20 minutes.

four　While the chops are cooking, make the gremolata. Mix together the parsley, sage, lemon rind, and garlic.

five　To serve, transfer the chops to a warmed serving plate and keep them warm. Boil the sauce to reduce if necessary, then pour it over the chops and spoon some of the gremolata over each one.

Preparation time **10 minutes**　Cooking time **15 minutes**
Total time **25 minutes**　*Serves 4*

Venetian calf's liver

one　Heat half of the butter and half of the oil in a large skillet, add the onions, and sauté for 10 minutes. Do not allow to brown. Remove the onions and set aside.

two　Season the liver on both sides with salt and pepper.

three　Add the remaining oil and butter to the pan. When it is foaming, add the liver and cook on high heat for 2 minutes on each side, or longer if you do not like your liver pink in the middle. Remove the liver and place on a warmed serving plate.

four　Allow the skillet to heat for a few seconds, then add the wine and return the onions to the pan. Boil rapidly to reduce for 1 minute, then stir in the parsley and pour the sauce over the liver. Serve immediately.

4 tablespoons butter
2 tablespoons olive oil
2 onions, finely sliced
4 x 6 oz. pieces thinly sliced calf's liver
½ cup red wine
1 tablespoon finely chopped parsley
salt and pepper

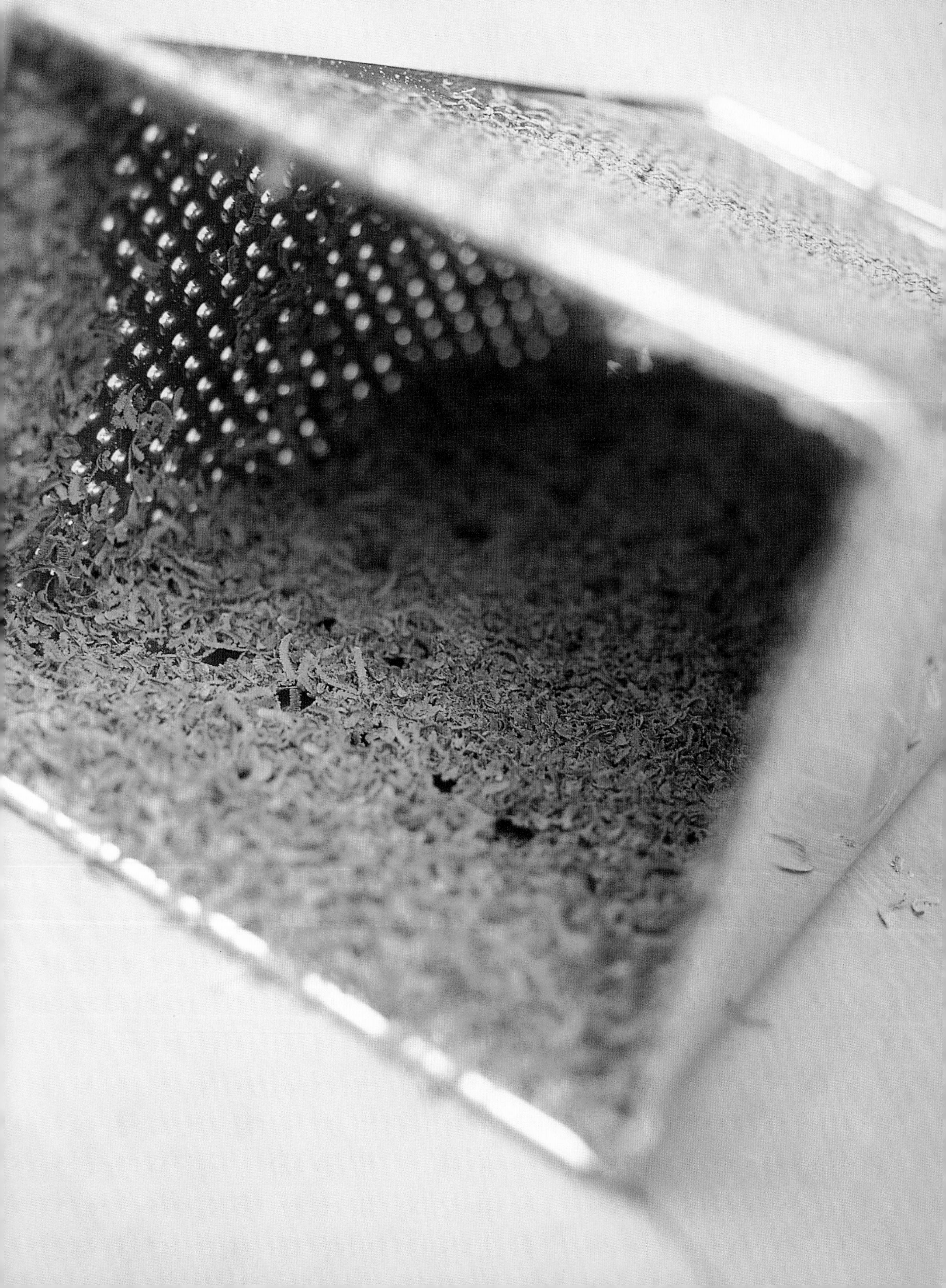

Desserts

This chapter includes some classic Italian desserts as well as some unusual new ideas, including sweet and chocolate risottos.

Preparation time **15 minutes, plus chilling**   Total time **15 minutes**   *Serves 4*

tiramisu with raspberry surprise

4 tablespoons very strong espresso coffee
2 tablespoons grappa or brandy
10 ladyfingers
4 oz. raspberries
6 oz. mascarpone cheese
2 eggs, separated
¼ cup powdered sugar
1 oz. dark chocolate

This dish is best made the night before so that it can set completely.

one   Combine the coffee and grappa or brandy. Dip the ladyfingers into the liquid to coat them evenly, then arrange them on a small shallow dish or a serving platter, pouring any excess liquid over. Sprinkle the raspberries evenly over the soaked ladyfingers.

two   In a bowl, whisk together the mascarpone, egg yolks, and powdered sugar until smooth and well blended.

three   In another bowl, whisk the egg whites until stiff and glossy, then fold together the egg whites and the mascarpone mixture until well blended.

four   Spoon the mixture over the ladyfingers and smooth the surface. Finely grate the chocolate straight onto the mixture. Cover and chill until set.

Preparation time **5 minutes**
Cooking time **10 minutes**
Total time **15 minutes**   *Serves 4*

zabaglione

4 egg yolks
¼ cup plus 2 tablespoons sugar, plus extra for frosting the glasses
grated rind of ½ lemon
½ teaspoon ground cinnamon, plus extra to decorate
1 drop vanilla extract
½ cup Marsala
4 oz. fruit (such as peaches, apricots, berries), sliced

one   Place the egg yolks, sugar, lemon rind, cinnamon, and vanilla extract in a heatproof bowl and beat with an electric mixer until thick, pale, and creamy.

two   Place the bowl over a saucepan of simmering water and continue beating. Slowly add the Marsala and beat until the mixture is warm, frothy, and thick.

three   To serve, dip the rims of 4 glasses in water, then in sugar to frost them. Divide the fruit among the glasses, then spoon in the zabaglione. To serve, dust with a little extra cinnamon.

Italian trifle

one   Spread the ladyfingers with the jam and arrange in a glass serving bowl. Sprinkle the Marsala or sherry over and add half of the blueberries.

two   Mix a little milk with the cornstarch to make a smooth paste. Stir the paste into the rest of the milk. Pour into a saucepan and bring to a boil, stirring all the time, as the milk will thicken; when it is boiling and smooth, remove it from the heat.

three   Whisk the egg yolks and sugar in a large bowl until they are light and creamy. Add the thickened milk to the beaten egg mixture, whisking all the time. Blend well and pour over the blueberries, then top with the remaining blueberries. Allow to cool.

four   Softly whip the cream and spread over the trifle, then top with the grated chocolate.

This dessert is very good if made the night before to allow all the flavors to blend together.

8 ladyfingers
2 tablespoons blueberry jam
¼ cup Marsala or sherry
8 oz. blueberries
1 cup milk
1 tablespoon cornstarch
2 egg yolks
2 tablespoons sugar
1 cup whipping cream
2 oz. chocolate, grated

blood orange granita

one   Using a sharp knife, cut off the top and bottom of the oranges, then cut away the pith and peel. Working over a bowl to catch the juice, cut the segments out of the oranges and squeeze any excess juice from each one.

two   Strain the juice in a saucepan, add the sugar, and heat until it has dissolved.

three   Place the orange flesh in a food processor or blender and blend until smooth. Mix in the juice and pour into ice cube trays to freeze.

four   When you serve the granita, first chill the serving dishes for a short time in the freezer. To serve, remove the granita ice cubes from the freezer, put them in the food processor or blender, and blend for 30 seconds, then transfer the granita to the serving dishes and serve immediately.

2 lb. blood oranges
1 cup sugar

Preparation time **5 minutes**   Cooking time **25 minutes**
Oven temperature **350°F**   Total time **30 minutes**   *Serves 4*

panettone pudding

4 tablespoons butter
5 slices panettone
a little apricot jam for
spreading
1 cup milk
1 cup heavy cream
2 eggs
1 egg yolk
¼ cup brown sugar, plus
extra for the crust

one   Butter a 4-cup ovenproof dish. Spread the panettone slices with the apricot jam and cut them into triangles or rectangles. Place in the buttered dish; try to arrange them in overlapping layers.

two   Put the milk and cream into a saucepan and bring gently to a boil.

three   Whisk together the eggs, egg yolk, and sugar in a bowl until creamy and fluffy. Continue whisking and slowly add the hot milk and cream. When it is all combined, carefully pour it over the panettone; make sure that it is all covered by the custard mixture. Sprinkle with a little extra sugar to make a nice crunchy crust.

four   Fill a roasting pan with boiling water, place the panettone pudding in this bain marie, and bake in a preheated oven, 350°F, for 25 minutes or until the custard is set.

Preparation time **10 minutes**
Cooking time **10 minutes**
Total time **20 minutes**
Serves 4

caramelized orange and pineapple

4 oranges
¾ cup sugar
½ cup water
1 small pineapple

one   With a very sharp knife, remove the rind from 2 of the oranges and slice it into very fine strips. Place the rind in a pan of boiling water and simmer for 2 minutes. Remove and drain well.

two   Put the sugar and water into a saucepan and heat gently, swishing the pan constantly until the sugar is dissolved. Increase the heat and boil the syrup until it turns a golden brown. Be careful not to overcook the caramel, as it continues to cook in the pan once it is golden as it has reached such a high temperature. If it does get too dark, carefully add 2 tablespoons of water. Stand back when adding the water as the caramel spits. When it is golden, place it to one side, ready to pour over the fruit.

three   To peel the oranges, cut a slice off the top and bottom of each one, then place the orange on one of these cut sides and cut with a knife around the side of the orange, cutting away the skin and pith. Cut across the orange into about 6–7 slices.

four   To prepare the pineapple, cut off the top and bottom and slice away the skin from top to bottom. Make sure that you remove the "eyes" close to the skin. Cut the pineapple into quarters and remove the core. Cut into slices.

five   Make alternate layers of orange and pineapple in a heatproof dish, sprinkle with the orange rind, pour the caramel over, and let stand until required.

This dish is very good if prepared up to the cooking stage the night before and then kept in the refrigerator. This allows the panettone to soak up the custard.

Preparation time **5 minutes**   Cooking time **25 minutes**
Oven temperature **350°F**   Total time **30 minutes**   *Serves 4–6*

lemon polenta syrup cake

12 tablespoons butter
¾ cup sugar
4 oz. ground almonds
2 oz. flaked almonds
½ teaspoon vanilla extract
2 large eggs
finely grated rind and juice of
1 lemon
¾ cup polenta flour
½ teaspoon baking powder
light cream, to serve
Syrup:
grated rind and juice of 2 lemons
¼ cup sugar
2 tablespoons of water

one   Line a 6-inch cake pan with waxed paper.

two   Beat together the butter and sugar until light and creamy.
Add the ground and flaked almonds, vanilla extract, and eggs,
and mix well. Add the lemon rind and juice, polenta, and baking
powder, and mix well. Spoon into the prepared pan and bake in
a preheated oven, 350°F, for 25 minutes.

three   While the cake is cooking, make the syrup. Put the
lemon rind and juice, sugar, and water in a saucepan and heat
through. Spoon over the cake as soon as it comes out of the
oven. Allow the syrup to drizzle through. Serve the cake hot or
cold with light cream.

Preparation time **10 minutes**   Cooking time **12 minutes**
Oven temperature **425°F**
Total time **22 minutes**   *Serves 4*

almond soufflés

1 tablespoon butter, plus extra
for greasing
¼ cup all-purpose flour, plus
extra for dusting
¾ cup plus 2 tablespoons milk
3 oz. ground almonds
3 eggs, separated
⅛ cup sugar
6 tablespoons Amaretto
4 macaroons, crushed
powdered sugar, to serve

one   Butter 4 small soufflé dishes and dust with flour.

two   Melt the butter in a small saucepan, add the flour, and stir to a smooth
paste. Slowly pour in the milk, stirring constantly, to make a smooth sauce.
Add the ground almonds and egg yolks; mix well and rapidly. Do not leave the
pan on the heat. Add the sugar and Amaretto and mix well.

three   Quickly whisk the egg whites until stiff. Fold in the almond sauce,
then quickly fold in the crushed macaroons.

four   Divide the mixture between the prepared soufflé dishes and cook in a
preheated oven, 425°F, for about 12 minutes until risen and golden. Dust with
powdered sugar and serve immediately.

Preparation time **5 minutes**   Cooking time **15 minutes**
Oven temperature **400°F**   Total time **20 minutes**   *Serves 4*

baked peaches with almonds and honey

4 tablespoons butter, plus extra for the dish
4 large ripe peaches, halved and pits removed
2 oz. flaked almonds
4 tablespoons honey
a little ground cinnamon
crème fraîche, to serve

one   Butter a shallow baking dish, large enough to hold
8 peach halves.

two   Place the peaches in the baking dish, skin side down.
Dot with butter, sprinkle with the almonds, drizzle with the
honey, and dust with cinnamon.

three   Bake the peaches at the top of a preheated oven,
400°F, for 10–15 minutes. You want to get a little color into the
peaches and lightly brown the almonds.

four   Serve the peaches with the juices drizzled over and
topped with a spoonful of crème fraîche.

Preparation time **5 minutes**   Cooking time **20 minutes**   Total time **25 minutes**   *Serves 4*

poached pears with honey and cinnamon

rind and juice of 1 lemon
1½ cups red wine
½ cup plus 2 tablespoons water
5 tablespoons clear honey
1 mace blade
1 cinnamon stick
6 cloves
4 ripe pears, peeled
thick yogurt, to serve

one   Put the lemon rind and juice, red wine,
water, honey, mace, cinnamon, and cloves into a
saucepan and bring to a gentle boil.

two   Add the pears and simmer for 10 minutes,
or until they are soft, turning them occasionally.

three   Remove the pears with a slotted spoon
and set aside. Transfer the liquid to a saucepan
with a larger surface area. Place the pan on high
heat and boil rapidly to make a rich, thick, sticky
syrup. Spoon the liquid over the pears and serve
with thick yogurt.

Preparation time **10 minutes** Cooking time **15 minutes**
Oven temperature **350°F**
Total time **25 minutes** *Makes approximately 16*

almond macaroons

These macaroons are delicious served with coffee. They can be stored in an airtight container for up to 10 days.

4 oz. ground almonds
⅔ cup sugar
2 large egg whites
½ teaspoon almond extract

one Line 3 baking sheets with waxed paper.

two Mix the ground almonds and sugar thoroughly. Whisk the egg whites and almond extract until stiff and glossy. Add the ground almond mixture to the egg whites and fold in until evenly blended.

three Using a small teaspoon, place spoonfuls of the mixture on the baking sheets, leaving space between them so they can expand slightly. Place the baking sheets in a preheated oven, 350°F, and bake for 15 minutes. The macaroons should be golden and slightly firm.

four Remove the macaroons from the oven and let stand for 5 minutes to cool and set. Lift them off the waxed paper with a thin spatula and allow to cool completely.

Preparation time **5 minutes**
Cooking time **10 minutes**
Total time **15 minutes** *Serves 8*

almond brittle

Serve this almond brittle with ice cream or good strong coffee. Store it in an airtight container.

8 oz. blanched almonds
1 cup sugar

one Line a baking sheet with waxed paper.

two Put the almonds on a broiler pan and place under a preheated broiler until lightly brown. Allow to cool a little, then chop coarsely.

three Heat a non-stick skillet over moderate heat, add the sugar, and allow to melt into caramel. Be careful that the heat is not too high, or the caramel will burn and have a very bitter taste. Add the almonds and mix in, then pour the almond brittle onto the prepared baking sheet.

four Leave the almond brittle to cool, then break it into small pieces.

Serve the chocolate risotto in coffee cups for an Italian flavor. Use a good-quality dark chocolate with a high percentage of cocoa solids—at least 70%.

Preparation time **5 minutes**   Cooking time **20 minutes**
Total time **25 minutes**   *Serves 4*

chocolate risotto

one   Put the milk and sugar into a saucepan and heat to simmering point.

two   Melt the butter in a heavy-bottomed saucepan, add the rice, and stir well to coat the grains.

three   Add a ladleful of hot milk and stir well. When the rice has absorbed the milk, add another ladleful. Continue to stir and add the milk until it is all absorbed. The rice should be slightly al dente and with a creamy sauce.

four   Finally, add the hazelnuts, golden raisins, and grated chocolate, and mix quickly. Serve decorated with a little grated chocolate. Try not to over-mix the chocolate, as the marbled effect looks good. For a special treat add a splash of brandy just before serving. Decorate with grated chocolate.

2 cups milk
⅛ cup sugar
4 tablespoons butter
4 oz. arborio or carnaroli rice
2 oz. hazelnuts, toasted and chopped
2 oz. golden raisins
4 oz. good quality dark chocolate, grated
splash of brandy (optional)
grated chocolate, to decorate

Preparation time **5 minutes**   Cooking time **20 minutes**   Total time **25 minutes**   *Serves 4*

sweet risotto

This unusual sweet risotto is not unlike a creamy rice pudding, but with more flavor.

2 cups milk
⅛ cup sugar
½ teaspoon vanilla extract
4 tablespoons butter
finely grated rind of 1 lemon
4 oz. arborio or carnaroli rice
2 oz. raisins
2 oz. toasted flaked almonds
3 tablespoons honey

one   Put the milk, sugar, and vanilla extract into a saucepan and heat to simmering point, then turn off the heat.

two   Melt the butter in a heavy-bottomed saucepan, add the lemon rind and rice, and mix well to coat the grains.

three   Add the raisins and a ladleful of hot milk and stir well. When the rice has absorbed the milk, add another ladleful. Continue to stir and keep adding the milk until it is all absorbed. The rice should be slightly al dente and with a creamy sauce.

four   Serve in individual dishes, sprinkled with toasted almonds and drizzled with honey.

Index

Author's acknowledgments

I really want to say a big thank you to all the people I have worked with: I believe that we all learn from each other and become inspired, thus new creations evolve. I have worked with chefs both fantastic and not so fantastic; they all helped as they made me think and influenced my direction. When we are young it is all about direction and choice, and I am happy with the choices I made as I decided to travel and work. Through this work in various countries, I meet all sorts of chefs and use ingredients that influence my cooking. This book is full of my Italian influences, and the three things that are close to my heart where food is concerned: the essence of speed in preparation, a clean modern approach, and the importance of fresh ingredients. I would also like to thank Nicky Hill at Octopus who gave me the opportunity to write this book, which has been a challenge and a pleasure; my partner David Tatton, who has been my taster and tester with his hungry but critical palate; and David Loftus, who took the photos, which I am sure you will agree capture my three rules of cooking. Thank you, everyone.

fran warde